Comments on THE GLOBAL FORUM
and *Earth Conference One*

"The Global Forum was without doubt the most significant gathering I have attended in a lifetime. It changed my life irreversibly. . . . Anuradha Vittachi's book is a wonderfully accurate and feeling account of what happened at Oxford."
—James Lovelock, author of *Gaia: A New Look at Life on Earth*

"When we talk about global crisis, or a crisis of humanity, we cannot blame a few politicians, a few fanatics or a few troublemakers. The whole of humanity has a responsibility because this is our business. I call this a sense of universal responsibility."
—His Holiness the Dalai Lama

"The value of the Earth Conference is to recognize that we are one species living on one small, vulnerable, fragile planet. We must reach out to embrace everybody on the planet or we will destroy ourselves. We must become a global civilization."
—Carl Sagan, author of *Cosmos*

"The Oxford Conference will be interpreted by history as a maturation of humankind's shared sense of responsibility for stewardship of our globe. It models the kind of communication on which we will have to depend if we are to preserve our land, air, water, and wildlife for the generations who follow us."
—Senator Dave Durenberger

"At the Oxford Conference the people involved had set aside ego and their own personal agendas. I was impressed with their commitment to work for the common cause of world peace and continuity of life."
—Chief Oren R. Lyons, Faithkeeper of the Onondaga Council, Iroquois Confederacy

"An extraordinary combination of uncommon human beings has produced a work as compelling and timely as the issue they set out to address: our survival on a threatened planet. For those who have long thought about humanity's relationship to the natural world, and for those who are just beginning to explore what it means to be part of a living universe, *Earth Conference One* is an important document."
—Norman Lear, television producer

"This is such a small thing I ask of all of you at this Forum: Go back to your countries. Do what you must do to protect life."
—**Mother Teresa**

"To call for a conference of spiritual and parliamentary leaders is something entirely new. The threats to the survival of humanity, other forms of life, and to the environment, are breaking down many ancient and artificial barriers. There is a great hope in a conference of this kind, standing as it does for a new determination to find answers to intractable global problems at local, national, and worldwide levels."
—**Rev. James Parks Morton, Dean of the Cathedral of Saint John the Divine**

"It is when thinking of our children that the challenges of survival become most immediate. To address the problems that lie in store for them will demand nothing less than the joining of forces of people from all countries and all walks of life. This book is about a meeting that offers us a glimpse of what this kind of alliance might be like. It reveals the essence of a world that is unfolding through people who, in spite of their national, religious, political and professional diversity, share a common vision for a brighter future for our children."
—**James P. Grant, Executive Director of UNICEF**

"This Forum is clearly one of those occasions when leaders in different areas of life can come together to reflect upon the urgency of their own historical predicament. It takes place at a time when, in secular terms, it is not just human survival but the whole earth which is in some evident peril."
—**Dr. Robert Runci, Archbishop of Canterbury**

"*Earth Conference One* accurately reflects the reality and the emotion of the Oxford Global Survival Conference. That the Conference was a great gathering of people with many different religious and political beliefs was self-evident. What was more important, however, was that all these people were about to establish between them a unity of opinion and purpose aimed at the target of global survival. I congratulate Anuradha Vittachi on encapsulating the spirit of the Conference as well as its message of action and hope."
—**Sir Charles Morrison, Member of Parliament, United Kingdom**

NEW SCIENCE LIBRARY

offers traditional topics from a present perspective. Its aim is the enrichment of both the scientific and the spiritual views of the world through their dialogue and exchange. The series encompasses a wide range of subjects, with special interest in the following three areas:

COGNITIVE SCIENCE. Cognitive science investigates the mind and mental processes through a blend of disciplines that includes artificial intelligence, neuroscience, linguistics, philosophy, and psychology. To these approaches, New Science Library adds anthropology and meditative techniques.

SCIENCE AND SPIRITUALITY. This area includes comparative or integrative studies relating any of the modern hard sciences with all of the great spiritual and wisdom traditions, rituals, and practices. Of particular interest are contributions from mathematics, the physical sciences, and biology.

ECOLOGY AND GLOBAL CONCERNS. Ecology is inseparable from cultural, political, and economic global concerns since the human species is a part of the complex and interdependent web of life and cannot ultimately dominate it.

New Science Library is an imprint of Shambhala Publications.

EDITORS   Jeremy W. Hayward
           Francisco J. Varela
           Ken Wilber

Earth Conference One

Sharing a Vision for Our Planet

Anuradha Vittachi

NEW SCIENCE LIBRARY
Shambhala
Boston & Shaftesbury
1989

NEW SCIENCE LIBRARY
An imprint of
Shambhala Publications
Horticultural Hall
300 Massachusetts Avenue
Boston, Massachusetts 02115

Shambhala Publications
The Old School House
The Courtyard, Bell Street
Shaftesbury, Dorset SP7 8BP

9 8 7 6 5 4 3 2 1

First Edition

Printed in the United States of America on acid-free paper

Distributed in the United States by Random House
and in Canada by Random House of Canada Ltd.

Library of Congress Cataloging-in-Publication Data
Vittachi, Anuradha.
  Earth Conference one : sharing a vision for our planet / Anuradha
Vittachi.
    p. cm.
  ISBN 0-87773-503-4
  1. Human ecology—Congresses. 2. Pollution—Congresses.
3. Environmental protection—Congresses. 4. Nuclear warfare—
Environmental aspects—Congresses. I. Earth Conference (1st :
1988: Oxford University) II. Title.
GF3.V57 1989   89-8253
304.2—dc20   CIP

Cover photograph: Courtesy of Gillman & Soame, Oxford.

Turn back, dull heart,
and find life's center out. . . .

King Lear

To my father,
whose heart is never dull

Contents

Foreword

THE Global Forum of Spiritual and Parliamentary Leaders on Human Survival was without doubt the most significant gathering I have attended in a lifetime. It changed my life irreversibly, as it must have done the lives of many of the other delegates and participants. I knew during the weeks before the meeting when I was preparing my address that it was unusual; after all, how often does one share a platform with leaders of the world's religions, parliamentarians, scientists, and theologians? But I had no notion that the meeting was to mark a divide between the old years, dominated by tragic and pointless tribal confrontations between people, with the ever-present threat of violence, from the childish spite of terrorism to the horrors of nuclear devastation, to the new years, where our prime concern would be as members of the human race confronted by global-scale environmental threats of our own making and with little time to do anything but seek in common some way of countering them.

I think that the Forum set the scene for the recognition by national leaders that we are part of the Earth and that the looming threat of global environmental changes, which are the result of agriculture and industry worldwide, warns of a greater danger than thermonuclear war, or narrowly based, purely human concerns.

Over the past few decades we have come to realize that we have one home, our planet. It was significant and appropriate that the Oxford Town Hall, where the meeting was held, was dominated in a visual sense by a vast photograph of the Earth seen from space. That stunning vision of a blue sphere wrapped in cloud, so unlike any other planet, enthralled the eyes of the first astronauts, and all of us vicariously. Indeed, there were the cosmonaut Valentina Tereshkova with us at the Forum to tell us how that vision moved them and played a part in bringing them before us. It is the fate of such visions to become in a way clichés, but in truth we can no more ignore the symbolism of the living planet seen from above than we can ignore the Cross or even the *Mona Lisa*.

Within a few months of the Global Forum at Oxford, peace had broken out all over the world. The fact that the six-hundred-year-old tribal war of northern Ireland continued its monstrous irrelevance only served to monitor and emphasize the larger change of heart. Politicians of the West and East, the North and South, were at last able to talk of planetary problems, not just human ones. It seemed as if being forced to think of the future of our planet instead of just ourselves induced a larger form of ecumenism, one that encompassed not just the human religions but also the commonwealth of species that form the living part of the Earth itself.

Anuradha Vittachi's book is a wonderfully accurate and feeling account of what happened in Oxford. It captured that nuance, that first feeling that the real agenda of the meeting was unconscious, something that took form as participants and attenders gathered and talked in small groups around the ancient quadrangles of that splendid university. It must have been no easy task to distinguish the real meeting of minds from the spoken words that sometimes seemed as out of date as an old newspaper found lining a drawer. The rarity of such expressions and the solid substance of the Forum are a tribute to the vision of one man, Akio Matsumura, who unstintedly and with great dedication gave so much of his life and time to its fulfilment.

Meetings, I often think, are like those fancy decorated cakes encrusted with towers and palaces and zoos of tame animals made of inedible solid sugar, whereas the real cake—the food for thought, where flavors have mingled in the dark—lies beneath. The prepared papers of most meetings all too often reflect the indigestible clichés, the tired, oft-repeated statements of past speeches delivered to a different audience. These are the icing; the solid meat comes from unrehearsed thought and is given voice in the corridors and quads away from the meeting halls. The Global Forum rose well above this level with several remarkable speeches, but the only expression of the true agenda was the speech by Oren Lyons, Chief of the Turtle Clan of the Onondaga Nation, who recalled the wise words spoken a century ago by Chief Seattle.

The Global Forum did not end with the departure of the coaches from Oxford on April 15, 1988. For many of us it still goes on as a new and thrilling way of life, a rewarding and purposeful communion that has sustained us and set our minds and hearts on the true task ahead: to ensure not just human survival, but the survival of all life through living in harmony with the Earth itself.

JAMES LOVELOCK

Preface

A planet stands at the edge of extinction, doomed by ecological breakdown and threats of war. An emergency council is called of the planet's leaders: can their world be saved? A hundred spiritual leaders and a hundred political leaders speed from all corners of the world in an attempt to solve the biggest crisis they have ever faced. Science fiction? No. The planet is the Earth, and the time is now.

A hundred spiritual leaders, including the Dalai Lama, Mother Teresa, and the Archbishop of Canterbury, recognized the global emergency and agreed to meet a hundred parliamentarians representing every continent to share their vision of how the planet could be saved. They met for a week of intense deliberation at the Global Survival Conference, held at Oxford's Christ Church College in April 1988, supported by scientists of vision and commitment to global survival, such as Carl Sagan, James Lovelock, and Evguenij Velikhov (Mikhail Gorbachev's chief advisor on disarmanent), as well as international journalists, filmmakers, and educators eager to spread their thoughts around the world. It was the first time in the planet's history that such a meeting had taken place between the leaders of historically hostile realms, the spiritual and the temporal. At this unique interfaith and intercultural meeting Moslem leaders rubbed shoulders with Jewish rabbis; a Pakistani politician sat beside an Indian prince.

What happened when they met? Did they defend their separate corners and protect their egos? Or did they actually listen to each other and shift from their old positions? Did the meeting bring more despair, or were there new insights?

This book records the substance of that spiritually charged week. James Lovelock described it as "the most important meeting I have ever attended in my life." No one left unchanged. In the pages that follow, I have recorded my own experience of the gathering; I have tried to uncover what made it so different from most and to formulate those principles for better human behavior that emerged gradually from the gathering during the course of the week. What follows, therefore, is in no way an official report but a personal statement. Each person who was there had a unique experience. I can only describe mine—and my understanding, however faulty, of what I imagine others meant when they spoke to me.

"It is always an impertinence to claim to write about a community," Bikhu Parekh once wrote. But "despite the difficulties, it helps us to know how it is held together and what makes it a distinct and unique community." The Oxford Global Survival Conference was certainly a distinct and unique community, and, despite the difficulties, I hope this book will convey something of the extraordinarily inspiring quality that held this community together and could, perhaps, be a template for the planet as a whole.

Acknowledgments

My first thanks must go to the participants at the Oxford Conference who shared their thoughts with me so generously—often at unsocial hours, well before breakfast or long after midnight. Not everyone who gave their time is mentioned by name in the book, sometimes in order to protect confidentiality, but every contribution has been deeply appreciated.

Special thanks are due to Akio and Maki Matsumura, to Cecile Reyes, and also to Sam Koo, Jamie Linton, Wilfrid Grenville-Grey, and everyone else at the Global Forum office who put so much energy and heart into making both the conference and the book possible. My thanks also to Fritjof Capra for his clarity, and to Chris and Ewa Robertson for their key insights into the nature of inner and outer change.

I owe thanks also to my family: to my older daughter Devi, for her lucidity as well as her secretarial help; to my younger daughter Pudi, for freeing me from the worst household tasks while I was writing; and to my husband, Peter Armstrong, for the intellectual discipline which helped give the book its shape—but most of all for being the sort of human beings the planet needs: warm, just, and open to dreams.

1 These Days of Mortal Peril

> The danger is that if you just bring together a few
> politicians and a few religious leaders, they will
> say some nice things, and you will say some nice
> things, and you will agree—and then you will go
> home.
>
> METROPOLITAN PAULOS MAR GREGORIOS

"WHY did they put that snap up there?"

The question came from an Indian professor of philosophy
sitting next to me. He was looking up at a photograph of the Earth
taken from space, a thirty-foot enlargement that had been rigged
up high above the platform. Throughout the week this portrait of
the Earth floated above us, serene and beautiful. Clearly, the
organizers of the Oxford Global Survival Conference hoped the
image of the Earth would remind us, without a word, of the peace
and wholeness we were longing for.

My neighbor understood the intention of the organizers very
well. But I knew why he objected. The technological expertise that
allowed the photograph to be taken in space and transported to us
here with such apparent ease and confidence should not mislead
us into thinking that some technological wizardry would solve the
problems of global survival. However serene the portrait of the
Earth might look from space, achieving that serenity on terra firma
was not going to be a simple matter.

Indeed, from late Monday afternoon, when the conference
opened, speaker after speaker drew attention to the huge and
multiplying problems in the world. A waterfall of catastrophes
tumbled from the platform: acid rain, deforestation, the tear in the
ozone layer, nuclear war, the debt crisis, terrorism, famine . . . In
addition to these external dangers, we heard about internal threats

1

to the human psyche: materialism, marital violence, pornography, drug abuse, teenage alienation. The world was being torn apart outside and in.

If a patient had this many disorders, a doctor would despair about where to begin. It was the same for us. What should our priorities be? Should we focus on political problems, spiritual starvation, environmental pollution? Adding to our pressure was the knowledge that we had to move fast. Each of the Earth's illnesses was serious enough to put her on the emergency list. Whichever disorder we focused on, another could erupt and kill her.

Some of the spiritual and temporal leaders at the conference identified the threat of nuclear war as the Earth's most pressing disorder. His Eminence Cardinal Franz Koenig of Vienna reminded us in the opening meditation on Monday afternoon that "more than fifty thousand atom bombs are stored in the world's arsenals, enough to destroy the world fifty times over." Japan's then–prime minister Takeo Fukuda sent a message to the conference in which he said that, of all his many worries about the future of the planet, the nuclear threat was uppermost. "While some moves are seen in both blocs to eradicate the idiocy of nuclear arms expansion, it is still in the initial stage," he said. "There is still no guarantee that these nuclear weapons will not be used. I shudder at the thought." The American astronomer, Carl Sagan, offered a dramatic metaphor to illustrate the danger of nuclear escalation: "The confrontation between the United States and the Soviet Union reminds me of two implacable enemies who have locked themselves into a room that is awash in gasoline. One of them has, let us say, twelve thousand wooden matches in his pockets, and the other nearly 11,500. They are each desperately engaged in procuring more matches—to make them 'safe.' " Sagan's Russian counterpart at the conference, Evguenij Velikhov, vice president of the Soviet Academy of Sciences, was equally worried: he devoted his address almost entirely to the nuclear issue.

The nuclear threat did not, however, have absolute priority at the conference. There was a rival concern: the ecological breakdown of the biosphere. James Parks Morton, dean of the Church of St. John the Divine in New York City and one of the conference's organizers, emphasized the threat to the ozone layer and the rain forests in his talk, while making it clear that these were only symptoms of a planet under threat. It was "the whole business: the biosphere, the entire planet in danger" that concerned him. Even if we didn't blow ourselves up, many of the conference delegates pointed out, the continuing degradation of the Earth would lead to annihilation.

If the ozone layer continued to tear, for example, that would be enough to erase humanity through death by cancer and by starvation. Dr. Sagan explained exactly how the process would take place. Mars, he said, unlike the Earth, has no sunscreen, so

> the surface layer of Mars is fried by ultraviolet light from the Sun. [But] high up in the atmosphere, twenty-five kilometers or so, where the air is very thin, the Earth has a fine layer of ozone. Were the entire ozone layer brought down into this room, at the pressure and temperature of this room, it would be one quarter of a millimeter thick. It is a very thin and fragile screen, a very delicate protection against ultraviolet light from the Sun.
>
> Through the development of a seemingly benign chemical, the chlorofluorocarbons, the protective ozone layer is now thinning. These chlorofluorocarbons were developed as refrigerants, as propellants in aerosal spray cans, in the development of plastic foams. Their great virtue was that they were chemically unreactive, so that they could do, it was thought, no harm. But ozone is so reactive that the chlorofluorocarbons simply accumulate until they find themselves high in the atmosphere, where they chemically combine with the ozone, removing it and letting the ultraviolet light in.
>
> The net result of an increase in ultraviolet light at the surface of the Earth has been discussed, but in my view not on the proper grounds. It's been discussed as dangerous because it will cause an increase in skin cancer. Well, it will cause an increase in skin cancer especially in light-skinned people. Dark-skinned people are so very nicely protected by melanin that they do not have as much to worry about. There is a kind of cosmic

justice in this: the light-skinned people develop the chlorofluorocarbons, which then preferentially give skin cancer to light-skinned people: the dark-skinned people who had nothing to do with the invention are protected.

However, there is not much cosmic justice along these lines because, as Sagan went on to say,

> The principal dangers are not skin cancer. The big danger is that we are at the top of some great ecological pyramid, some vast food chain; and at the base of that food chain are microbes that are vulnerable to increase in ultraviolet light.
>
> It's clearest in the oceanic ecosystem: at the very top of the ocean there are small light-harvesting micro-organisms called phyton plankton, one-celled plants. They don't have much in the way of resources. They process light into food and they are then eaten by little one-celled animals, called zoo plankton. They in turn are eaten by little invertebrates including krill, a kind of shrimp, and they in turn are eaten by little fish; little fish are eaten by bigger fish. The bigger fish are eaten by dolphins, who are eaten by nobody except ultraviolet radiation. Something similar, although we are more ignorant about the food chains on land, is likely to be the case on land.

Nuclear war, environmental breakdown leading to cancer and starvation: that seemed to be enough for the conference to deal with, but there was more. The international financial system, we heard, was precariously poised. It could collapse at any moment. Money—that commodity whose chief characteristic in ordinary times seemed to be its reassuring solidity, its frustrating but ultimately comforting finiteness—could go crazy, crazier than in the Great Depression of the 1930s, and inflate into meaningless-ness before shrivelling like an untied balloon. Money is now the hard language of the international business world; words are pliable and can be twisted, but putting your money where your mouth is reassures everyone that you mean what you say. If money were to keep changing its meaning, the rules of economic and political dealing would founder.

Who would suffer the most? The poor, of course, for whom the value of each penny is sacrosanct. In their budgets, they have no margin for inflationary flux. Professor Mawupe Vovor, former president of the National Assembly of Togo, was worried about the effect of financial instability on developing countries, which would not be able to cope with a further devaluation of their incomes. He warned of "dangerous stagnation and even a regression in Third World development, increasing the international debt of the poorest of countries."

Prime Minister Fukuda added his fears: "Since the first oil crisis of fourteen years ago, the old order of the world economy collapsed and the new path is yet to be established. Starting with the United States, all countries are confronted with major difficulties. In particular, the developing world is suffering from protracted economic stagnation and the most grave external debt problem. No one can be certain that none of these debtor countries will bankrupt. The economic uncertainties in each of these countries will trigger social and political chaos."

In case we should forget what financial distress already means to poor people, James Grant of UNICEF, in a speech read out by his deputy, Marco Vianello-Chiodo, told us that "thirty-eight thousand children die each day, and a comparable number are crippled for life—the vast majority from causes for which we have long since discovered low-cost cures or preventions." If the remedies are already known and they are so cheap, why do the children die? Because their families are too poor to afford even these five-cent remedies, or they live in countries too poor to distribute them where they are most needed. As a result of this poverty, Jim Grant informed us, a child dies unnecessarily every two seconds. If poverty deepened further, how many more children would be crippled by disease and malnutrition, or die lingering deaths? The developing world is already spending a quarter of its export revenues repaying the interest on its debts to the industrialized world, cutting back on family health and welfare budgets in order to meet these payments. If inflation were to rise further and the interest repayments to rise, even more children would die.

We were reminded by yet another participant that 20 percent of humanity—a billion people—suffer daily hunger despite the enormous wealth that exists in the world. Most of us at the

5

conference are shielded from the experience of such poverty. How could we become sensitized to the reality that so many of our fellow human beings experience every day, since that sensitization must be the first step in motivating us to change an obscene inequality? One of the observers at the conference, Masatoshi Kohno, a Rissho Kosei-kai Buddhist, told me that he, in common with the other 6.5 million members of this Buddhist lay organization, practised voluntary fasting. Three days a month, every month, they skipped a meal and contributed the cost of these meals to helping the poor—for example, by buying trees to be planted in Nepal, to counter soil erosion. Even more important than the financial contribution was the sense of solidarity with the hungry that it awakened in the well-fed: "As you see," he said, pointing to his thin frame, "I'm very skinny. If I just skip breakfast, I am feeling dizzy by lunchtime. It is a way to be symbolically with the people who are hungry all the time."

I thought of the times I have fasted, and how difficult I have found it. I could hardly bear to think beyond the minor discomfort of missing a meal or two to the pain of real hunger. With a shock I remembered an incident in Sri Lanka when I was about eight or nine years old. I heard a man shouting in the road outside our house. I ran to the window and saw the man, bones protruding, staggering from one side of the road to the other and crying out in a voice too desperate for pride, "Hungry! Hungry!" I edged towards him, terrified, and saw him collapse, writhing in pain on the tarmac.

There are a billion people hungry like this, every day; a thousand million innocent human beings, guilty of no crime but poverty. And as the environment deteriorates, there will be less food available to feed the world's people, not more. So what was the conference going to focus on—nuclear war, the ozone problem, debt, or hunger?

Several of the participants added population growth as a major problem, while still others referred to terrorism, violence in general, or the widespread alienation that led people to blot out the miseries they saw with escapist addictions like drink or drugs or by bombarding their senses with electronic flak.

A vast array of issues had been set before the conference. By the time the opening session ended on Monday evening, we were left with a picture of a planet falling apart before our horrified eyes. Nor was there any hiding place; no country was safe from danger. Even if the government of the country we lived in were determined to take good care of its people and its environment, the carelessness of other countries would damage us. Leaflets available at the conference told us about Scandinavian lakes and forests, for example, being damaged by acid rain from Britain; it was estimated that eighteen thousand Scandinavian lakes are dead or dying as a direct result of acid rains. Our life support systems were fragmenting all around us as we watched—and the longer we stood staring, the faster we saw the rate of fragmentation accelerating. Professor Vovor summed up the times we live in as "these days of mortal peril and infinite disorder."

Human beings have always been faced with mortal danger, of course: people in the Bronze Age or the Middle Ages knew catastrophe. But in those days, although catastrophe came to the group we lived in, or to ourselves and a clutch of neighboring groups beyond the hill, or on the other side of the river, or even on the other side of the ocean, humanity would continue to thrive. What we are now facing is a full-scale and imminent wiping out of our entire human race—and much of the biosphere along with us.

By the end of the first day, the conference hall was filled with a sense of urgency. An Oxford undergraduate, who was helping the conference organisers as a volunteer, said, "I had heard of these problems before, but I'd never registered them. Hearing them repeated over and over like this by forceful speakers makes you really take them in." In a paper called "The Secrets of Successful Grassroots Action," the key to success was described as passing on "compelling information." The information we heard at the conference, some which we had heard and half taken in before, suddenly did seem compelling—perhaps because the conference had put together so many aspects of a planet in trouble. Any one of these problems we might feel able to put aside to consider another day, but how can you put aside a deluge? After what we had heard, we could no longer retreat comfortably into the manageable problems of our everyday lives, with our attention to global survival shrunken to a flickering glance at a news item.

This raising of the participants' consciousness was a powerful act in itself, at a time when governments and news media were still placing their attention elsewhere. It was clear by the end of the first evening of the conference that we had to act urgently to save our planet. The question we faced was no longer Should we act, but How? We needed only to know where to begin.

Like others at the conference, I felt a desperate need for some port in this stormy sea where I could stop and take stock of what was happening, find some sense of direction through this chaos. Dr. Robert Runcie, the Archbishop of Canterbury, put his finger on the need many of us felt when he said we were "confronted by a search for meaning in the human enterprise."

That was exactly the point. To get successfully through any crisis, any period of suffering, we need to perceive its nature and meaning. A woman who feels repeatedly dizzy and sick will naturally be anxious about her health—until she realizes she is pregnant. That new meaning, that change of perception alters everything: her attitude toward her symptoms and the way she deals with them. In the same way, we needed to see the meaning in the changes that were taking place on the planet.

Were we living in a world that was breaking down haphazardly—or was there some underlying meaning in all these symptoms of breakdown? Perhaps the world was pregnant with a new and worthwhile future—something worth the suffering of this painful childbirth. Or were we merely seeing the signs of irreversible decay? Even if the process were only negative, we still needed to know its meaning in order to halt the downward slide.

From the platform came calls for unity, which demonstrated the longing for a single conceptual "bag" to contain all the jangling problems that had been presented to us. Were these problems really disparate or were they somehow connected? That was the key question. Were they symptoms of a deeper malaise—like a person with AIDS who has thereby lost his immunity to secondary infections? If so, we needed not only to keep the secondary infections from overwhelming the patient, but urgently to make a more searching diagnosis of the primary illness.

As a therapist, I was accustomed to stepping back to find meaning. A patient would often appear buzzing with a mass of problems—most of which were indications of a deeper, unconscious problem. It was my task to see, together with the patient, the underlying situation that was trying to show itself through the symptoms. To cure a symptom prematurely would be to erase a clue.

An African delegate who looked uncomfortable during a long and detailed group debate about the nuts and bolts of nuclear disarmament made the point firmly: "Discussing the disarmament issue is not all we need for peace and survival," he said. "We need to deepen our diagnosis."

A conference called specifically to discuss disarmament, or saving the ozone layer, could discuss how best to solve that single issue—and if they managed it, everyone could go home satisfied. But at the Oxford Conference, global survival was our brief. Nothing short of that would do. So it seemed that we, too, had to be like a therapist: to look at the spate of disasters as symptoms of breakdown—and get from them a sense of the underlying problem. We needed not so much to cure the individual symptoms as to ask ourselves why they had appeared—why these particular problems? Why now? How were they linked? Nothing short of finding the meaning behind this multiple crisis would do, even if we failed in the attempt. So meaning, rather than piecemeal solutions, was what we were here to find: a shift in perception.

The very multiplicity of the problems we had been presented with that first afternoon had shown us that, since we were facing a hydra-headed monster, cutting off one head wouldn't make enough difference to save humanity. Too many other heads would still be there, slavering over us. While we heroically killed the torn-ozone head, the debt-crisis maw would be opening wide behind us. And even if we swung round expertly to deal that a blow, the nuclear warfare head would almost certainly get us. If we stayed focused on disarmament, millions of fellow humans would go on dying a slow and agonized death from hunger and disease.

It dawned on me for the first time that the principle of wholeness might be what the myth of the hydra was there to express. Until the conference I had never thought of its meaning, just dimly remembered it as a blood-and-guts fighting story. But the experience of the conference on that first day had brought home the pointlessness of getting attached to solving one fragment of a problem as though it were unconnected to a larger whole. And that was also why we had needed to come together from all over the world to look at global survival. It wasn't enough for just some of us to look at some parts of the problems of survival—we were there together as representatives from the whole world to enlarge the context of our looking, to perceive a large enough meaning to encompass the whole planet.

And then I remembered that the myth had gone on to give us a further warning: cutting off a head, without understanding that we must burn it off at the root, resulted in the growth of two heads. In our haste and anxiety for practical results, we might be tempted to rejoice when someone cuts off a hydra head: but this hero would in fact have doubled the danger. It was time to stop waving our swords short-sightedly at one head or another, making matters worse by our superficial, isolated solutions; the conference had reminded us that we needed to pause—and find the heart of the hydra.

2 The Tree of Life

> Instead of production, primarily, we have to think
> of sustainability. Instead of dominating nature, we
> have to acknowledge that nature is our source and
> best teacher. Instead of understanding the world
> in parts, we need to think about the whole.
>
> WES JACKSON

TUESDAY morning. I looked out of my study window a few
minutes after seven, expecting to see a silent, romantic Oxford in
the early light. My room at Christ Church overlooked Peckwater
Quad, where Evelyn Waugh had set the early chapters of his
classic novel *Brideshead Revisited*—it wasn't hard to imagine
Waugh's young aristocrats sauntering tipsily across the grassy
quadrangle.

In fact, what I saw resembled nothing that Peckwater Quad
had ever witnessed before. In the center of the formal English
garden stood the high priest of the Sacred Forest of Togo. Despite
the chill of an April morning, the brightly coloured cotton robes
he wore exposed a gleaming black shoulder and most of his upper
body. Beside him, similarly dressed, stood a Togolese tribal chief.
Their feet were bare.

As I raced to get dressed and run downstairs to the quad, I
missed the explanation of the ceremony translated for the circle of
onlookers by a young Frenchman in a beret; the fragments of the
ritual that I glimpsed included a bowl of leafy herbs, doused and
blessed and handed out to the onlookers who sipped reverentially.

What did the ceremony mean? Since leaves were important,
and since the conductor of the ritual was the high priest of the
Sacred Forest, I imagined that the ceremony was celebrating trees
in some way. Another startled delegate who had come down to
watch whispered to me: "I thought I was pretty ecumenical. I've
thrown myself willingly into Jewish rituals, Christian and Buddhist

11

ceremonies, Hindu festivals—but I find it hard to witness this ceremony without a faintly anthropological tinge. Trees? They don't hold a big place in my idea of religion." But at the end of the day, the same observer said, "Now I realize how central the Sacred Forest ceremony is." For trees unexpectedly played a starring role that morning.

James Lovelock, the first speaker of the day, centered his speech on trees, although he is best known for his scientific research on atmosphere—the electron capture detector, for example, one of his many inventions, had been directly responsible for the discovery of the global distribution of chlorofluorocarbons in the atmosphere. And his most famous contribution to our store of knowledge, the Gaia hypothesis, also arose out of his reflections on the nature of the Earth's atmosphere. In *Gaia—A Way of Knowing,* Lovelock speaks about how he came to frame the Gaia hypothesis: "The thought kept recurring: how is it that the Earth keeps so constant an atmospheric composition when it is made up of highly reactive gases? Still more puzzling was the question of how such an unstable atmosphere could be perfectly suited in composition for life. It was then that I began to wonder if it could be that the air is not just an environment for life but is also a part of life itself." In other words, "The physical and chemical condition of the surface of the Earth, of the atmosphere and of the oceans has been, and is, actively made fit and comfortable by the presence of life itself . . . in contrast to the conventional wisdom which held that life adapted to the planetary conditions as it, and they, evolved their separate ways." So Lovelock sees the Earth not as a dead rock that we have carved out to make a habitable cave, but as a living entity responding to the other forms of life in its biosphere—indeed, systematically enabling the other forms of life to exist. The name Gaia was suggested by Lovelock's neighbor, the novelist William Golding, after the Greek Earth goddess (also known as *Ge*—from which *geography* and *geology* are derived).

Despite all this interest in the atmosphere, on Tuesday morning Lovelock chose trees as his theme. He began with a heartfelt tribute to a man who loved them:

My father was born in 1872 near Wantage, some fifteen miles from here. He was that kind of countryman who felt himself to be part of the natural world. For him there were no weeds, pests or vermin. Everything alive was there, in his view, for a purpose. He had an immense respect for trees and referred to them as the noblest form of plant life.

With this in mind I would like to make trees the theme of my address today. To start with, imagine that you are standing on the stump of a giant redwood tree that has just been felled. It was a vast tree weighing over two thousand tons and over one hundred meters tall, a spire of lignin and cellulose. The tree started life two thousand years ago.

A strange thing about such a tree is that during its life nearly all of it is dead wood. As a tree grows there is just a thin skin of living tissue around the circumference. The wood inside is dead as is the bark that protects the delicate tissue. More than 97 percent of the tree we stand on was dead before it was cut down.

Now in this way a tree is very like the Earth itself. Around the circumference on the surface of the Earth is a thin skin of living tissue of which both the trees and we humans are a part. All of the rocks beneath our feet and the air above us is of course dead. But the air and the rocks are either the direct products of life or have been greatly modified by its presence. Is it possible that the Earth is alive like the tree?

It was the view from space, about twenty years ago, that showed us how beautiful and how seemly was our planet when seen in its entirety. The Earth was also seen from space in invisible wavelengths through the sensors of scientific instruments and their view made some of us re-examine our theories about the nature of the Earth. It led my colleague and friend Lynn Margulis and me to propose that the Earth itself was indeed in some ways alive like the tree, alive at least to the extent that it could regulate its climate and chemical composition. We called the idea Gaia after the old name for the Earth.

A tree is in many ways a living model of the Earth.

Indeed, some single trees of the tropical forests are almost complete ecosystems in themselves. They shelter a vast range of species from microbes to large animals, to say nothing of numerous plants growing on their branches. Those tropical trees are nearly as self-sufficient as the Earth. They recycle almost all the nutritious elements within their canopy and with the other trees sustain the climate and the composition of the forest.

My view of the Earth sees a self-sustaining system called Gaia like one of those forest trees. Although some of my colleagues in science are beginning to take it seriously as a theory to test, most prefer to see the Earth as just a ball of rock moistened by the oceans, a piece of planetary real estate that we have inherited. We and the rest of life are just passengers. Life may have altered the environment or have coevolved with it, as by putting oxygen in the air, but they see this as no more than the act of passengers who, on a long sea voyage, may decorate their cabins.

If mainstream science is right and the Earth is like this, then to survive it might not matter what we do so long as we do not foul it so much as to hazard ourselves and our crops and livestock. But what if, instead, the Earth is a vast living organism? In such a living system species are expendable. If a species, such as humans, adversely affects the environment, then in time it will be eliminated—with no more pity than is shown by the microbrain of an ICBM on course to its target. If the Earth is like this, then to survive we face the hard task of reintegrating creation, of learning again to be part of the Earth and not separate from it.

The idea of the Earth as a living, breathing organism comes as a shock when you first hear it. It reminded me of those stories where explorers have been sitting on logs that suddenly move and reveal themselves to be crocodiles. There is a shocked transformation in our attitudes. If the log is a log, then we feel we can treat it as we please, casually exploiting it as an insensate object: we can sit on it, carve our initials on it, burn it. But if we perceive it as a crocodile, a living creature, then we become aware that we cannot treat it casually, if not for its sake, then at least for our own safety. It is the same with the Earth. We have been treating her as if she were a lump of insensate matter. But what if she were not a rock, but Gaia?

Gaia. Goddess Earth. Mother Earth. What if "matter" were to be uncovered and revealed as "mother"? Etymologically, the words are connected. What if we are children of the Earth, umbilically linked to Gaia, rather than alien conquerors of mere territory?

Whether we accepted the idea of a living Earth literally or only metaphorically, the crucial insight Lovelock offered us was the importance of "learning again to be part of the Earth and not separate from it." While we saw ourselves as separate from the Earth we could behave badly towards it, as if the damage we did to it didn't matter in itself and didn't rebound on us. Blinded by this illusion, we were able to pollute rivers, stain the sea and the air; we could strip the fields of their fertility and tear down the forest trees—thinking all the while only of our immediate profit, our "high productivity." But as soon as we saw the Earth and ourselves as part of the same whole, then we could see that we can no more strip the Earth and remain unaffected than we could strip off our skin and not feel the pain.

Lovelock did more than to help us see the Earth as a living whole; he began the process of reintegrating us into that whole, by wondering aloud with us how this conceptual separation had come about and how we could relearn the process of seeing ourselves as part of the Earth. His answer was to put spiritual awareness back into scientific knowledge—an inner meaning into outer information: "If we choose to go this way," he said, "the change of heart and mind needed will include also the reintegration of religion and science. In Newton's time he was able to say 'theology is the queen of the sciences.' I happen to think that, although science has progressed vastly since Newton, it has also moved a long way in the wrong direction. Scientists had to reject the bad side of medieval religion: superstition, dogmatism, and intolerance. Unfortunately, as with most revolutions, we scientists merely exchanged one set of dogma for another. What we threw out was soul."

James Lovelock saw as the danger our tendency to draw a

magic circle around humans, separating us from other forms of life and demoting them into second place. This hierarchical divisiveness and distancing allows humans to treat the rest of creation unlovingly. Love, as we all know, draws us near one another, it reconnects us; separation allows domination and tyranny. If we are to reconnect to the Earth, Lovelock reminded us, we need to reawaken our love for her.

> The life of a scientist used to be that of a natural philosopher, closely in touch with the real world. It was a life both deeply sensuous and deeply religious—truly in touch with the world. You see, curiosity is the principal motivation of the natural philosopher and curiosity also is an intimate part of the process of loving. Being curious about and getting to know a person or the natural world leads to a loving relationship.
>
> I sometimes wonder if the loss of soul from science could be the result of sensory deprivation, a consequence of the fact that 95 percent of us now live in cities. How can you love the living world if you can no longer hear bird song through the noise of traffic, or smell the sweetness of fresh air? How can we wonder about God and the universe if we never see the stars because of the city lights? If you think this to be exaggeration, think back to when you last lay in a meadow in the sunshine and smelt the fragrant thyme and heard and saw the larks soaring and singing. Think back to the last night you looked up into the deep blue black of a sky clear enough to see the Milky Way, the congregation of stars, our galaxy.
>
> The attraction of the city is seductive. Socrates said that nothing of interest happened outside its walls, and that was two thousand years ago. But city life is a soap opera that never ends. It reinforces and strengthens the heresy of humanism, that narcissistic belief that nothing important happens that is not a human interest.
>
> City living corrupts. It gives a false sense of priority over environmental hazards. We become inordinately obsessed about personal mortality, especially about

death from cancer. Most citizens, when asked, list nuclear radiation and ozone depletion as the most serious environmental hazards. They tend to ignore the consequences of greenhouse gas accumulation, agricultural excess, and forest clearance. Yet in fact these less personal hazards can kill just as certainly. Sadly, we are the witnesses of the disintegration of creation without realizing that we are the cause.

We were beginning to understand some of the consequences of our human narcissism. Because we are so wrapped up in ourselves, we tend to see the rest of the world as put there for our use. We worry about the damage we do only when we see its consequences as directly threatening to us. Reducing damage for the sake of life itself doesn't count—unless we are among those people who have made ahimsa (the law of reverence for, and nonviolence to, every form of life) our philosophy. So until we see the damage we do ricocheting back on us, we carry on plundering and ravaging, exploiting the Earth in the name of technological efficiency and progress.

A Survival International bulletin at the conference bookstall offered an example of violent "efficiency" at work in Sarawak, Malaysia. Here, the Dayak peoples are mounting human barricades to stop logging companies with high-tech machinery damaging their lands. They explain, "Our life was not easy, but we lived it content. Now the logging companies turn rivers into muddy streams and the jungle into devastation. The fish cannot survive and wild animals will not live. You take away our livelihood and threaten our very lives. We want our ancestral land back. We can use it in a wiser way."

Narcissistic domination is what the modern culture of success has lauded; our winners are the heroes who grab more and grab faster, with little attention to the consequences of rapid plunder; we praise people who focus on the acquisitiveness of the individual or the clan without an awareness of the whole. But sustainability—the opposite ideal—is beginning to filter back, but slowly. In *Six Assumptions That Have Shaped American Agriculture*, Wes Jackson wrote, "Instead of production, primarily, we have to think of sustainability. Instead of dominating nature, we have to acknowledge that nature is our source and best teacher." At the Oxford conference, participants were beginning to remember these very old values. We saw that we needed to take time to be receptive, not always prescriptive; to learn lessons from observing the Earth's reality instead of imposing our "reality" onto it.

A psychotherapist observing the conference described our egocentric domination of Mother Earth with an analogy from psychology:

> We have been behaving like a five-month-old infant who doesn't want to grow up. In his narcissistic babyhood, the baby sees its mother as existing only to look after him. She has no being, no purpose, other than that. She comes and goes when he demands comfort, or food, or warmth, as far as the baby is concerned. He is the be-all and the end-all of the universe. But as the baby grows older, when he is about five or six months old, he realizes he is not the center and periphery of the universe; he has limits, and there are others beyond those limits. It is a hard lesson, and he may be angry and frightened that he is no longer a god—a tyrannical god that has so far screamed for his mother to come at once because he "owns" her. It is a necessary learning, if he is to have a healthy relationship with his surroundings. Unfortunately, not every baby learns this lesson— there are quite a few middle-aged men around who haven't stopped tyrannizing the provisioning mother.

What humans are beginning to realize—or rather, to remember— is that we are not infant gods who own Mother Earth and can scream for unlimited sustenance from her as our right. We are beginning the hard way to learn our limits. Economists are fond of telling us that we must recognize the limits of the Earth. At the Oxford Conference we had the opportunity to see it another way: the limits we need to learn about are our own. Our nineteenth-century ancestors liked drawing evolutionary hierarchies with humans at the top of the tree. We have, it seems, perched there for long enough. Now it is time for us to climb down and join the other species on the ground—around the tree, looking at it, rather than on top of it, looking away from it. Father Tom Berry, director of religious research at the Riverside Center, said in a simple phrase that caught the imagination of many of the participants, it was time we recognized that we are "a specie among species."

We were beginning to see that we are part of an ecological web. We are not the weavers of the web; and we have no right to make it or break it; we are but one strand in the web, neither more important nor less than any other. But when we (who are merely a part of creation) see ourselves as "the be-all and end-all of the universe" we make two kinds of mistake: first, we behave with greedy destructiveness; and second, because we are linked to everything else in the web, we set in motion a chain reaction of ecological catastrophe. James Lovelock provided a dramatic illustration of this process:

> The humid tropics are both a habitat for humans and the heartland of Gaia. The habitat is being removed at a ruthless pace. In the First World we try to justify the preservation of tropical forests on the feeble grounds that they are the home of rare species of plants and animals, even of plants containing drugs that could cure cancer. They may do. But they offer so much more than this. Through their capacity to evaporate vast volumes of water vapour the forests serve to keep them cool and moist by wearing a sunshade of white reflecting clouds and by bringing the rain that sustains them. Their replacement by crude cattle farming could precipitate a disaster for the billions of the poor in the Third World. Imagine the human suffering, the guilt, and the political consequences of a Sahel drought throughout the tropics, to say nothing of the secondary climatic consequences here in the temperate regions.

He referred to the Panama Canal to provide a further example of a negative chain reaction: "The canal climbs over the isthmus of Panama through a series of locks. The entire system is powered and kept filled with water by the abundant rainfall of that humid region. But the rain and the trees of the forests are part of a single system. Now that the forests are being destroyed to make cattle ranches, the rain is declining, and soon it may be too little to sustain and power the Canal." And he makes the point again

19

about our narcissistic short-sightedness: we do not appreciate the intrinsic value of the rain forests—we only begin to value them when we see the consequences of cutting them down ricocheting on human commerce. "Somehow the fact that this great work of engineering is threatened by an insatiable desire for beef brings home most clearly the consequences of burning away the skin of the Earth to the thick-skinned denizens of the cities."

Lovelock's speech struck home to many people in the conference. Perhaps it was because he had done what Wangari Maathai of Kenya's Green Belt Movement said we all needed to do: to "raise consciousness to the level which moves people to do the right things for the environment because their hearts have become touched and their minds convinced. To do the right thing because it is the only logical thing to do." Lovelock had stirred in his listeners something of the love for the natural world that he himself felt with such passion, and had awakened a dramatic consciousness of the planet as one living organism. The Earth was suddenly subject rather than object.

Wangari Maathai, the next speaker, also described the Earth as if it were alive—but only metaphorically so. "I came to Oxford," she said, "because my mind and my heart are not at peace. How can they be at peace when I see all these wounds and all these bleeding sores everywhere?" After the precise, reflective Professor Lovelock with his off-stage shyness, Dr. Maathai presented the conference with a very different personality. She delivered her speech ringingly; she was forceful and lyrical, calling for a personal commitment to heal human divisions. But she, too, focused on trees:

> The realization that other forms of life depend on trees and other green plants came late in the afternoon of my life. When I realized that the green form of life can live without us but that we cannot live without it, I committed myself to its preservation. I knew then that destroying it is suicidal. I knew then that plants, and the soil in which they grow, are more precious than silver and gold. But because of their abundance we take them for granted, we cut them, burn them, poison them, and treat them with little respect. When their number

reaches the minimal critical point, disasters follow, and we rush to prayers, grain silos, and international fora. We act as if we have discovered something completely unexpected. [The result is that] the Earth is being stripped naked, abused, wounded, and left to bleed to death!

But to see the damage is not enough. The next step is to take personal and collective responsibility for it: "When we have seen all these calamaties, what have we done? Have we only asked, 'Who is doing such horrible things? Who is so cruel, so unjust, so ungodly?' Have we only asked, 'Is it the politicians, the rich, the poor, the West, the East, the North, the South, the women, the religions?' Who is responsible? For me personally, I know that I am responsible for some of it. I am sure that you are also responsible for some of it. We are all responsible for some of it directly or indirectly. We are all strangling the Earth."

It came as a relief to hear her speak like this. At other conferences, the problem on the table always seemed to be someone else's fault: if only "they" weren't so selfish, or so blind to "our" way of thinking, things would be all right. Sometimes it even seemed as if the chief purpose of these conferences was to deflect attention away from the participants having to alter their own lives in any way. So far, no one at the Oxford conference had indulged in this game.

Lovelock had already suggested that we all make a personal contribution by moderating the damage we do. He expected nothing drastic, just a willingness to cut down on "the three deadly c's—cars, cattle, and chainsaws. You don't have to be a puritan and ban them, just use them moderately." With typical modesty, he mentioned—as if it were nothing special—his own family's contribution: "For each of us there is an appropriate course of action. For us as a family this has meant planting about twenty thousand trees." Twenty *thousand* trees?

Wangari Maathai had also planted trees. The Green Belt Movement, which she helped develop, was founded by the National Council of Women of Kenya to curb desertification. It is a popular environmental movement with tree planting as its central activity, using local expertise. But it also has a more general purpose: to develop in its members a holistic approach to development issues. "Trees," according to the movement's literature, "have indeed become a symbol of hope and a living indicator of what needs to be done."

I asked Wangari Maathai one afternoon why she thought trees were such potent symbols for people. Sitting in the sunshine, we mulled over the idea and together began to put into words—I no longer remember who said what—what we had always unconsciously known about trees and their meaning for human beings. Later I elaborated on what we had said, adding snippets I had learned during the conference week.

A tree is something you can easily see is alive; even as a child, you know you can plant trees and watch them grow as you grow. And though they are strong and reliable, trees are vulnerable, like people; you can cut them, and see them spill their lifeblood. Trees catch disease, and trees die. Trees eat and drink and breathe; they seem to dance and speak. It is not difficult for humans to identify with trees. Trees are a bridge between the human and the vegetable kingdom.

The great beauty of trees makes us like to see them around us; we can appreciate easily that they are to be treasured and loved, apart from their practical uses. Unlike gold, which is valuable because it is rare, we know deeply that each tree is valuable for its own sake, even when there are many—just as each person is valuable, even though are five billion of us. When a tree is destroyed, people mourn. They felt the loss, like the loss of a person they have known.

It is easy to regard trees as scenery and forget they hold meanings we have only begun to discover. Trees regulate our rainwater and oxygen supplies; they hold fast the soil we need to plant our food; they provide fuel. So trees are the guardians of good water, good earth, good air, good fire. Their fruit provides us with nourishment and with sensuous experiences: if a freshly picked orange or a mango were not commonplace, how we would marvel at its irreplaceable taste.

Like a human, a tree mediates between heaven and earth, between spirit and matter, its head and arms reaching for the sky and its roots in the soil; and life courses through its veined body, just as it courses through the body of a human. Every religion seems to use a tree to link earthly growth with spiritual growth: there is a Tree of Life in so many traditions. In Judaism there is a Tree of Knowledge, and in Christianity the cross on which Jesus died is sometimes referred to as a tree. American Indians draw their medicine wheel around a tree. In Buddhism, Gautama Buddha received enlightenment under the Bo tree.

If we lived a life that valued and protected trees, it would be a life that also valued and protected us—and gave us great joy. A way of life that kills trees, our present way of life, kills us too, body and soul.

Dr. Maathai was a scientist, not a religious leader. But the most striking part of her speech from the platform was a vivid evocation of a simple, timeless spirituality. She offered a symbolic sketch of our common progress from birth to death—from "the Source" to our "return to dust." At these points, when we are in the arms of nature, locked in the immutable realities of mortality, we are all alike; in between, where we have the power to act independently, we do our best to create differences.

I am not a religious leader . . . but when I have searched deep into my person I have felt peace with the religious concept that I am indeed comprised of a part of me that will return to dust and a part of me that will return to the Source. I know about the dust, so I search for the Source. Where is this Source? Who knows the Source? Which is the way to the Source? I know that we must all sometimes meditate on the Source. All religions meditate on the Source. And yet, strangely, religion is one of our greatest divides. If the Source be the same, as indeed it must be, all of us and all religions meditate on the same Source. If this be so, why are formal religions a source of such great divides?

Naturally, these are all simple questions for the

simpleminded people like me and millions like me, everywhere on this planet Earth.

Now, as you know, politicians are always meditating on that part of us that returns to dust. They are concerned about where that part is to be (or is not to be) born. They are concerned that it is not stateless, that it acquires a good (not necessarily fair) share of the world resources, both within national boundaries and within the larger world. They are concerned that the nationals are not overrun by others stronger than themselves (but that they preferably overrun others) and that when they die they will have ensured continuity through sons and daughters of their own type.

Upon death, though, suddenly we all appear to have such a common end! Suddenly we are humbled to dust and to our common destiny. These are humbling thoughts that ought to unite us, for into this world we are all born . . . all from the same Source and from dust. And we leave this home called planet Earth humbled to dust and on toward the Source.

Before some of us became overcivilized and overdeveloped we lived closer to the Source and dust. Religion was a way of life rather than an occasional exercise on specified days and hours. Religious leaders were also political leaders—and when different, they worked very closely together for the common good of their followers.

But our inventions, discoveries, and conquests seem to necessitate that politicians and religious leaders walk separate ways because there are too many divides between them. And that is partly why we came to Oxford. We wish we could reduce the gap. It takes much courage to be willing to retrace the steps and to try to make a convergence of the minds and develop a partnership. But that we are all here is already a major success in that direction. The first steps, the most difficult steps, have already been taken.

Wangari Maathai left us with a sense of the oneness of humanity revealed. It is a oneness that we do not need to create laboriously, but a oneness that needs only to be uncovered and perceived; it is as intrinsic as the oneness of the planet seen from space, but hidden by the artificial divisions we construct in our egoistic progress through life. By these divisions, foolishly, humans try to elevate themselves one above another. And then, as Lovelock had shown us, humans also tried to elevate themselves above the rest of nature. We set our fists against each other and against the planet, forgetting that we are all on the same side.

Now, on the second day of the conference, we were beginning to see that the human-planet conflict was absurdly one-sided, that Gaia was not fighting us: we were creating the difficulties all by ourselves, like a child breaking his toys and screaming at his mother. The heartening corollary of all this was that if we did stop behaving like a spoiled child and looked at what Gaia was offering, we would see at once that she was on our side. Gaia herself reached constantly toward sustainability and life. We had an enormously powerful ally in her—as we would see when we stopped kicking the goddess in the shins.

Unnoticed beneath our human dramas, Gaia was silently struggling to save the biosphere. We weren't on our own, trying to calculate complicated ecological balances by ourselves against impossible natural forces. On the contrary, all we had to do was to stop perversely operating against Gaia's natural tendency to create an environment suited for life. We needed to come to our senses, quite literally, and let her show us how to live with her in harmony.

Since the opening of the conference our understanding had moved forward a good way. Instead of seeing a multiplicity of vying problems, the participants now had a sense of everything and everyone on the planet being deeply interconnected, operating as a dynamic, living system—with a spanner in its works. That spanner is the human ego, which clings to the false reality that it could—or should—dominate its surroundings. If it does manage to control its environment, the ego imagines, it will be secure and have everything it needs.

But this belief is a myth. On the contrary, the ego's attempt to control and dominate destroys the very security it longs for. As spiritual leaders have said for centuries, it is only when the ego renounces this desire to dominate and recognizes instead its place in Gaia's scheme that the ecosystem will work to everyone's advantage. Since everything is interconnected, humanity might then set in motion a positive chain reaction instead of the negative one it is triggering at present.

A pollutant, it has been said, is a resource in the wrong place. We are, at the moment, by misjudging our place, behaving like a pollutant rather than a resource. If we go on behaving egotistically, Gaia, as Lovelock said, may be forced to shrug us off to protect her own survival; she may "eliminate us . . . with no pity."

3 *Global Citizens*

> Sovereign states have been mankind's para-
> mount objects of worship during the last five thou-
> sand years; and these are goddesses which have
> demanded and received hecatombs of human sac-
> rifices.
>
> ARNOLD TOYNBEE

CARL Sagan, professor of astronomy and space sciences at Cor-
nell University, brought an attentive intellect to bear on every
proposition; he challenged everything, as fits a man whose role is
to be sure of his facts. He said to me one afternoon at the
conference, "It is clearly the obligation of scientists to speak the
truth. The moment we stop doing that, we've sold our birthright."

We rely on some people for vision ("the truth, never mind the
facts") and some for facts. On Sagan we felt we could rely not only
for facts, but also for imaginative metaphor. And, crucially, he
linked facts and metaphor to his vision of ethical change. He was
deeply concerned with moral, ethical behaviour—and love. "I have
a social obligation to speak out on subjects if I have some special
knowledge," he said. "And beyond this, I am a human being; I
have children, I have a grandchild, I have people I love." His
manner toward other people at the conference, courteous and
forthright, seemed to flow from his belief in love and responsibility.

Sagan explained in simple terms the environmental dangers
that most of us had heard rumors of but hadn't begun to understand—the "greenhouse effect," for example:

> To keep warm, to provide light, to secure energy
> for industry, humans have hit upon the idea of burning
> fossil fuels—wood, peat, coal, oil, natural gas. There
> has been an enormous amount of this fossil fuel re-
> source accumulated on the planet, and we have been

27

relentless in pursuing it. It has been the energy source for the technological revolution that has remade our civilization.

A consequence of burning the carbon in fossil fuels is to combine it with the oxygen in the air to make carbon dioxide. Carbon dioxide is invisible and odorless—but while it is invisible in ordinary light, the sort our eyes are good at, it is significantly opaque in the infrared part of the spectrum. If our eyes were good at a wavelength of ten microns in the infrared, this room would be pitch black. You could not see your finger in front of your nose. The more carbon dioxide that is put into the atmosphere, the more opaque the atmosphere is in the infrared part of the spectrum.

But the temperature of the Earth is determined by a balance between the amount of visible light that strikes and is absorbed by the ground and the amount of infrared radiation that the ground is able to radiate away to space. If the atmosphere becomes more opaque in the infrared, that radiation to space is impeded, the heat is held in, and the temperature of the Earth increases.

It is now very clear that the amount of carbon dioxide is increasing, and recently there has appeared the clear climatic signature that the temperature of the Earth is also increasing. . . . By the middle of the next century the Earth's surface temperature will have increased by several degrees centigrade. That doesn't sound very serious—only a few degrees centigrade. But a few degrees centigrade increase in the average temperature produces much larger and more significant local temperature changes.

Those were the known facts. Getting the facts clear and compelling is obviously essential if we are to make an informed response. Next, Sagan went on to explore the probable consequences that follow from these facts:

One prediction which is not considered wild and irresponsible is that, about the middle of the next century, the American midwest and the Soviet Ukraine will be converted into something approaching scrub desert. Since they are important granaries for the human species, this is a matter of some importance.

In addition, as the temperatures continue to increase, polar ice melts and the sea level rises. At projected rates of the burning of fossil fuels, sometime by the end of the next century there is the possibility of the collapse of the West Antarctic ice sheet. The resulting rise in sea level is so great as to inundate all coastal cities on the planet. This is a very serious set of possible consequences from the most benign human activity— started when our ancestors first burnt a piece of wood or a lump of coal.

This was a prediction based on what would happen if we continued on our present course. But naturally, if we change our course, the future will look different. However obvious this may seem, it is a point worth underlining: the danger of predictions is that people submit passively to the images they offer. Images, as conference delegates frequently pointed out, are powerful in their force. We can become victims of a nightmare vision of the future, mesmerised like a rabbit before a snake, instead of taking steps to change it. As Sagan put it, "Dreams are maps." We need to remember that we have the power to choose an alternative dream.

As the conference went on it was becoming clearer that the dangers confronting human survival were not mysterious acts of God or Nature but processes set in motion by human choices. Those choices could therefore be changed, and the time had come to change them. But we should change them according to our values. The moment of choice is crucial, for it is the moment where our values come into play. For example, if we hold protection from the enemy as our guiding value, we will presumably choose to continue on the path of arms dealing. If we hold reverence for life on Earth as our guiding value, then we will choose an opposite route.

A guiding value like the wish to cherish life needs to be powerfully felt. Otherwise there will not be enough motivation in us to combat the forces of inertia. Like the speakers before him, Dr. Sagan used his eloquence to stir in us heartfelt love for the

29

planet, describing the Earth tenderly as "one lovely, delicate planet, exquisitely sensitive to the depredations of humans."

The religious leaders had justified their belief in the sanctity of life by pointing heavenwards: since God had created the living world through his divine love, who were we to mistreat it? Sagan also looked heavenward, but he found there a different reason for reverence: "In the vast cosmos in which this world is embedded, it is, at least among the nearby worlds, the only possible home for humans, the only world graced by life."

We mustn't waste the Earth: that was the clear message. We wouldn't find another one on the cosmic shelf to replace it with if we were careless with this one. Carl Sagan made us feel stricken at the carelessness—the callousness—we had already displayed. We had been criminally wasteful:

> How much money has been spent on the Cold War since 1945? I will give you the figures for the United States; the Soviet figures are probably comparable. If we add up all the expenditures from 1945 until January of this coming year in 1988 dollars, the answer is ten trillion dollars. Ten trillion dollars, the United States has spent.
>
> What could you buy with 10 trillion dollars? The answer is everything—everything in the United States except the land; every skyscraper, house, ship, train, airplane, automobile, baby diaper, pencil. Everything could be purchased for ten trillion dollars.
>
> A business that spent its capital so recklessly and with so little effect would have been bankrupt long ago.

In contrast, he offered an electrifying example of money well-spent: "Smallpox has been eliminated from the planet: the cost was one hour of the global military budget." And he suggested some other ways the Soviet Union and the United States could have spent these trillions:

> For something like that amount of money we could have made major progress toward eliminating hunger and homelessness, infectious disease, illiteracy, igno-rance, poverty not just in the Soviet Union and the

United States, but worldwide. We could have helped to make the planet agriculturally self-sufficient, so each nation could feed its own people, so that humans could be responsible for their own lives and thereby have removed many of the causes of violence and war.

Also, for the tiniest fraction of that money, think what prodigies of human inventiveness could have been accomplished in art, architecture, medicine, science, and technology. I have talked a little about what could have been done with that amount of money, but it is of course unavailable because it has been already squandered. Nevertheless, the world spends every year one trillion dollars on armaments. In addition, the world spends on illegal narcotic drugs something like half a trillion dollars every year. That is capital otherwise unavailable to the human species. We have decided to spend it on war and drugs.

I think of the poorest 20 percent of the human species, the poorest billion people on the planet. It's as if in our own families we have decided to have a lavish feast, but there is a brother we don't like or haven't seen, or would prefer to ignore; and so, we let that brother starve in the midst of our feast. In any family on Earth that would be considered obscene behaviour.

What kind of species are we, if we permit that to happen? Every two seconds, as Jim Grant of UNICEF said, an avoidable infant death occurs on the planet. Every two seconds, so [snapping his fingers at two-second intervals] one now, there's another, there's another, there's another. Day and night, for weeks, months, years, babies are dying, one every two seconds, all over the planet; deaths that could have been prevented for the tiniest fraction of what we waste on war and drugs.

For something like three hundred billion dollars a year, enough money could be made available—not in gifts, but in appropriate technology; not in fish, but in fishhooks—to raise the standard of living sufficiently to

31

achieve some measure of a decent life for those billion poorest people on the planet.

That amount is less than the world spends on arms every four months.

It was obvious from what Sagan said that we could and must make new moral choices. From these new choices, new practicalities like those he had outlined could follow. But merely to understand the moral dimension, Sagan reminded us, is not enough. The practical dimension must be made to follow understanding; idealism is useless unless it is implemented. "We are able to make major social changes. What we do now is well within our power, but it cannot be done merely by hoping. It requires serious changes, not just in our way of thinking but in our way of doing. It requires political action."

That spiritual and ethical values must be manifested in reality with the aid of parliamentary skills was the principle that underpinned this conference. But political assent and political action are not the same thing. Politicians at a convivial conference may agree that changes congruent with a planetary morality should be made—but would they fight to put these changes into practice when they returned home and were confronted with political opponents who were less idealistic or, at the least, more parochial in their idealism? Not to mention commercial interests that use their economic clout to pin politicians into place. Imagine the political determination that would be needed to curb the oil industry.

Or take the greenhouse effect—its dangers may be taken up by politicians in power only if they have a private agenda: to use it as a stick to beat a coal industry that they dislike for political, not environmental, reasons, or because they have a vested interest in supporting the rival nuclear power industry (without considering how far this, too, is a huge risk to the environment).

Sagan pointed out that there would have to be agreement on a global scale to stop burning fossil fuels: "Notice that there is no local solution; that carbon dioxide put up by one country does not respect national sovereignty, does not remain within the national borders. It becomes a global issue." And the agreement would have to be long-term as well as worldwide: "Notice also that there is no short-term solution. Once the carbon dioxide is up into the atmosphere it is not possible to scrub it out on the kind of time scale that we are discussing."

But in political life we are not used to dealing with problems as worldwide, long-term issues. Spiritual and ethical leaders may see issues *sub specie aeternitatis* as a matter of course, but politicians typically choose to see only as far as the next election. And they are elected to guard the rights of the electorate within nation states, not beyond them. Appeals to look after the planet coming from outside the national boundaries are likely to be regarded with derision.

Carl Sagan took the example of China, which has the world's largest coal reserves: "China is in the process of an exponential increase in its [coal] industry. Will the United States and the Soviet Union go to China and say: Look, we recognize that we have done a lot of burning of fossil fuels, but now will you kindly not do the same thing yourself, because we have lately recognized that we have made a mistake?"

A further difficulty is that parliamentarians would be able to persuade us to stop burning fossil fuels only if they could suggest alternative sources of energy. Sagan saw solar energy and perhaps nuclear fusion as the most promising alternatives, but "they will be expensive to develop. They will not be affordable by the developing world without great aid by the developed world. There is thus a very important ethical issue involved in this matter. This is a technological problem whose answer has to be partly technological, but partly a change in the distribution of the wealth of the planet. The developed and developing countries are equally at risk."

So it will not be only China that will have to make a material sacrifice, but the West as well. Is the rich world willing to redistribute its wealth—to share it with the poor? The stark alternative to sharing money so that everyone can afford new energy sources, according to Sagan's scenario, may be to share death by drowning when the West Antarctic ice sheet collapses. Nevertheless, the rich may choose to clutch their money tightly to their bosoms while the waters rise.

Till now, having money has been seen as a key, perhaps the key, to survival. It is deeply embedded in our psyches that the more money we have, the better our chances of seeing seventy. And as this perception has been largely true, we have had a strong and logical incentive to clutch at money. Lectures on Gandhi-like frugality are irrelevant for most people: we have it stuck firmly in our minds that we must survive, and that to survive we need more, not less. But now the logic has been reversed; from now on, we are beginning to see, hoarding will lead to death and sharing will lead to self-preservation. Until we see this new logic with blinding clarity, we will not share. Why should we?

Was the real change, then, that had to come about in the world not a technological miracle but a psychological flip? A 180-degree change in the way people understand which path leads to survival? The notion that we need to let go of our materialism in order to find salvation is not new—it is found clearly stated by the founders of our religions—but now it appears in a literal form. By sharing our wealth we save not only our souls but our bodies.

Shortly after the conference, a participant lent me a copy of Arnold Toynbee's last work, the massive and poignant *Mankind and Mother Earth*. In this Toynbee wrote: "Since the thirteenth century, Western Man has professedly honoured Francesco Bernadone, the saint who renounced the inheritance of a lucrative family business. But the example that Western Man has actually followed has not been St. Francis's [but that of] the saint's father, Pietro Bernadone, the successful wholesale cloth-merchant."

In 1983 President Reagan confirmed Toynbee's sardonic perception without a blush: "What I want to see above all is that this country remains a country where someone can always get rich." Was this really the guiding value of the leader of the most powerful nation on the planet? Unless this shriveled belief in individual acquisitiveness gives way to a larger one—larger than the individual, larger than the nation—we will be holding a set of values whose context is too narrow for global survival.

Huddled in our nations, we not only have hoarded like misers, but have also felt it necessary to barricade ourselves and our hoarded treasures. Our ports are guarded from foreigners. Entry is discouraged. And we have firepower to protect our treasure from thieves—or to help us thieve our neighbor's treasure. As Dr. Maathai said, we are concerned that we are not overrun by others stronger than ourselves, but have no objection to overrunning others. Defensiveness and aggression—the military path to survival—is the path humankind has pursued for thousands of years; it is how one tribe has protected its wealth from another, and wealth has seemed the basis of survival. But aggression cannot solve the issue of ever-accumulating carbon dioxide. "Notice," said Sagan scathingly, "that there is no military solution to this problem."

The conference members laughed, in recognition that the time had come for a change of attitude. For the kinds of global problems we know we have facing us, no alternatives remain but those based on international cooperation. To wave the banners of national sovereignty, to be aggressive and mistrustful in the name of patriotism, is to call for global suicide.

Sagan had shown very clearly through his explanation of the carbon dioxide problem not only how interconnected the natural world is, but how these interconnections extend to human relationships. The way humans choose to think and feel about each other affects how we choose to act in the physical world, and these physical actions in turn affect the planet's ecological system.

So our bad behaviour towards each other is not just a political or social problem; it is an ecological problem also. Carl Sagan had shown us that for humans to have respectful relationships with each other is no longer a mere luxury, any more than having a respectful relationship to the environment is: both affect ecological survival. We need to say yes to a moral interhuman ecosystem as part of a well-run physical ecosystem. As one delegate put it, "We need a moral ecology." And another: "War is ecological breakdown in human terms."

Our interhuman amorality is as ecologically ruinous as would be the bad behavior of the seas or the volcanoes. But seas and volcanoes don't misbehave; they follow the orderly, if mysterious, patterns of nature. The latest findings of scientists researching "chaos theory" are beginning to show that even such apparently random effects as the shapes of clouds or the patterns of animal populations or even of rising cigarette smoke follow mathematical formulae. We had assumed disorder where we failed to understand the hidden order. But order lies everywhere, it seems, in the cosmos. Even the word *cosmos*, as the Archbishop of Canterbury reminded us in his speech to the conference, means "order." It is only humans, with our free will, who are disorderly.

In the last decade, humans have begun to edge towards a better appreciation of the relationship between humans and nature. Even fifteen years ago, the word *ecology* was barely known to the public, and Green political parties were laughed at as "green" in a less flattering sense. But social commentators now say frequently that we must become stewards of the Earth's physical riches. What the speakers at the conference were saying, however, went well beyond this "light green" concept of stewardship, to use a term coined by the Friends of the Earth. "Light greens," to put it flippantly, are interested in conserving scenery. But "dark greens" perceive the attitude of domination that manifests in our assault of nature also manifesting in our attitude toward people: if we come across people less powerful than ourselves, we tend to exploit or ignore them, rather than treat them as members of our human family. Thus, men use women, the rich enslave the poor, and industrial nations exploit the developing world. So, to be dark green is to apply the principle of sustainability rather than domination to the whole of the human world as well as to the natural world.

Two examples came to mind. Light green wildlife conservationists in the West worry about the extinction of the tiger. They mount campaigns to save tigers from the villagers who kill them, and because their campaigns are powerful the villagers' actions are sometimes made illegal. But the campaigners in the West do not live where tigers enter their backyards and maul and devour their children; the villagers do. To look after the tigers' right to live without simultaneously taking care of the villagers' right to live is to act with indulgence and sentimentality, not ecological wisdom.

The second example concerns fossil fuels. We must remember, before we jump to the conclusion that banning the burning of all fossil fuels will save us from the greenhouse effect, that firewood is the chief domestic fuel of the rural poor in most parts of the world. Are we, in the affluent nations, now going to point sanctimonious, "ecologically sound" fingers at people who scavenge bits of wood to cook their meager meals?

There is a photograph that I have been haunted by ever since I saw it eight years ago. On the right of the picture, bulging out at the viewer, is a huge oil truck, the first in a long line of oil trucks that curves back all the way to the horizon. On the left, in the scoop of the curve, is a woman bent double under a pile of twigs, staring haggardly at the camera. More vividly than words, that picture tells us of the way the principle of domination works: the massive trucks are for men—huge vats of fuel are being brought to them on wheels, ready to turn more wheels in factories, before the noxious gases are released to paint the sky. What energy and money is spent on providing this fuel for industry! But how much is spent on providing fuel for women? What fuel but firewood is there for them? Yet the survival of their family depends on their daily efforts at gathering fuel.

If and when national energy policies change, we must change them so that they provide energy for those that need it most— ordinary citizens around the world; for the danger is that, when fossil fuels are forbidden and superseded, leaders of the powerful industrial nation may focus on new sources of energy that are even more remote, technologically complex, and centralized—and even less accessible to the poor.

Carl Sagan suggested solar energy and nuclear fusion as possible future sources of energy. Wouldn't dependence on nuclear fusion merely widen the gap between the members of the human family who have and those who have not? It seemed to me that renewable sources—sun, wind, waves, geothermal energy— were worthier of exploration. Why should research into these technologies be seen as belonging to the underfunded do-gooder camp of appropriate technology for poor countries? If something is appropriate, it seems to me, it should be so because it is appropriate for people and appropriate for an ecologically sustainable planet, and therefore appropriate for everyone—"appropriate" should not mean "good enough for poor people."

So far the scientists at the conference had demonstrated that, both in the conduct of our relationships with each other and with our environment, humans have made the wrong choices: we have assaulted the Earth and our fellow humans, acting from attitudes of domination and control. But our eyes were now being opened to the consequences of those principles, and we were beginning to realize that we can make better choices, based on attitudes stemming from less rapacious parts of our psyche. It is not too late.

37

What, though, has kept us from making these life-sustaining choices till now? Our "identification horizons," said Sagan, have been too narrow.

> In our long wandering, the human species has increased its identification horizons. First our identification was only with the small itinerant band with which we wandered. The names of many cultures all over the world translate in their language to "the people"; they were human, and no one else was. As time has gone on, the identification horizons have expanded—from itinerant hunter-gatherer group, to tribe, to clan, to city-state, to nation, to superpower. I believe the key question is whether the identification horizons will continue to expand and embrace the entire planet before we manage to destroy ourselves.

In other words, we can save ourselves only if we choose to see that "we" are all of humanity. As long as we stay shrunken within a tribal awareness of who constitutes "us," the human race remains in peril; for then, beyond the limited area belonging to "us" lies the area populated by "them." We begin to arm ourselves against the enemy without, to feel secure, and they do the same in return, to feel secure from us. Eventually we find ourselves, as Dr. Sagan put it so graphically, in the situation of the two men locked in the room awash with gasoline, counting their matches.

The assumption on each side is, of course, that the other wants to impose their identity on them by means of imposing their belief system—for our sense of identity tends to be heavily dependent on the beliefs we hold. By clinging to our opinions, we think we know who we are. Thus, many Americans may believe that the U.S.S.R. wants everyone to believe in communism, just as many Soviets may believe that the U.S. wants everyone to believe in capitalism. The fear on each side is that they will lose their own identity and be submerged under the identity of the other. It is not unlike a man and a woman who are afraid to live together, in case either one loses their identity, submerging it under the powerful psychological reality of the other's beliefs. Fortunately, not everyone is too afraid of such domination, or humanity would end in one generation without the intervention of bombs or pollution.

Power has had a bad press lately. But as a North American Indian put it: "Your power is your essence." To be alive to our essence is to be empowered in ourselves, not necessarily to dominate one another. And for two people to pool their essence willingly from time to time is to create a fruitful union. Will there be as fruitful an urge to union among the tribes of the planet? Or will the tribal ego guard its individuality by keeping its barriers up too high to achieve union?

We must become global citizens, said Sagan. In a press conference at the Town Hall after his speech, he said he considers himself a "Globalist."

But is this too naive a hope, given our history of nationalism? How is this shift to be made, from a tribal to a global awareness? "The minimum requirement of any state," he said, "is that it should be dedicated to the survival of the human species." To go back to first principles: what is the chief responsibility of the state? To look after its members. Traditionally, the state has fulfilled this responsibility by looking within its own boundaries, giving priority to the needs of its own members and turning its back on the interests of other states. But we have reached a point now when we see that the state can best fulfill its responsibility by being more, not less, aware of the whole. It is not a matter of self-denial but of self-interest for us to become global citizens: "We have to become a global civilization." Paradoxically, in order to maintain our proper patriotism we must see globalism as its first duty.

It may still be naive to hope that everyone will see the logic of this argument. The fear of an external enemy is deeply rooted. Many of us have an "enemy complex," as Charlotte Waterlow, a historian and peace activist at the conference, put it. But it is not naive to recognize that holding onto the enemy complex is a course guaranteed to end in disaster. Nor is it naive to see that humanity has had a history of rapidly widening its circle of identification. It was only a century ago that Italy and Germany became unified as nations, redefining their tribal enemies as those who lived outside the new national boundary lines. If nations now take the next step and join to make an international world, then the enemy complex will be pushed off the edge of the planet. Where would the enemy then reside? On the neighboring planets?

Arnold Toynbee, like Sagan, saw the deadly limits of the inwardly turned nation:

> Local sovereign states are an awkward institution. They fall between two stools. Even a city-state . . . is far too large to be capable of being based socially on the personal relations in which people feel at home.
>
> On the other hand, the largest local state is still only one of a number of states of the same kind. Wherever and whenever there has been a set of local sovereign states juxtaposed with each other, they have always fallen into warfare with each other, and, in the past, this warfare has always ended in the imposition of peace by the forcible establishment of an empire embracing as much of the Oikoumene as had lain within the horizon of the liquidated set of warring states.

In nineteenth-century Europe, empire-building through the domination of one nation over another was considered a perfectly acceptable norm. Invading and swallowing up another nation was not considered morally wrong, according to Hannah Arendt, until the First World War. On the contrary, the bigger you grew your empire, the more righteous and superior you proved your nation's culture to be. In *Anna Karenina,* Tolstoy gives an example of a dinner-party conversation that reflects these nineteenth-century values:

> "I do not mean . . . that we should set about absorbing other nations on principle, but that it would come naturally if our population were larger."
>
> "That amounts to the same thing," Alexei Alexandrovitch replied. "In my opinion only a nation with a superior culture can hope to influence another. A culture that . . ."
>
> "That is precisely the question!" Pestsov interrupted. "To whom do you accord the preference? Which nation is to take the lead? Who will enforce its nationality on the others?"

But we don't have to continue this habit of one nation enforcing its culture on another in order to prove its superiority. Already in the twentieth century, it has caused damage enough. The First World War was triggered by Germany's wish to prove the worth of its identity as a new nation by territorial aggrandizement, and the Second World War by Hitler's need to redeem the national ego, battered by the first war. We can't go on playing this game of national ego-boosting. Charlotte Waterlow likened the psychological immaturity of present-day nations to that of a teenager going through his adolescent crisis. While searching for his identity, he often clings to his separateness from the family group, withdrawing behind sullen silences or acting aggressively. But with maturity, he comes to know who he is and can rejoin his family without fearing a loss of his identity. It is time, Charlotte Waterlow felt, for the nations to grow up, to get through their adolescent crises before the family is kicked to pieces.

As the Reverend Jesse Jackson has said, it is time to choose "cooperation, not co-annihilation." It means being mature enough as nations to have a sense of our national identity without having to bolster it up at the expense of others. We should no longer need to see everyone else as an enemy in order to make our national ego feel secure. We could let go the idea of the enemy and realize that we are both on the side of life, rather than two sides, each hoping for the death of the other. The present crisis could teach us at last to give up the empire-building solution as a hopelessly counterproductive route to national security, and to search for alternative ways to protect our future.

This was Toynbee's alternative: "The present-day global set of local sovereign states is not capable of keeping the peace, and it is also not capable of saving the biosphere's non-replaceable natural resources. . . . What has been needed for the last 5,000 years . . . is a global body politic composed of cells on the scale of the Neolithic-Age village-community—a scale on which the participants could be personally acquainted with each other, while each of them would also be a citizen of the world-state." In this vision, people would belong to two groups, one a subset of the other. The universal group would encompass the whole planet, and the smaller group would be about the size of the gathering at the Oxford conference. Perhaps that was the experiment we were, without realizing it, trying out at Oxford. We had come from all over the planet and knew ourselves, therefore, to be a group of citizens of the world; we were also a community the size of a Neolithic-Age village, intimately and urgently drawn together by our common need to solve the problems of global survival in just five days. The solution, then, that we had to offer our fellow citizens might not lie so much in the conclusions we came up with at the end of the conference as in the experience of living together like this, at once members of the world and members of an alert and caring village.

4   The Case against Technology

Stretch a bow to the very full,
And you will wish that you had stopped in time.
TAO TE CHING

At times during the conference it had sounded like technology was our real enemy. The carbon dioxide problem had arisen only because fossil fuels had been used to power the West's Industrial Revolution. The ozone layer had been ripped apart by the "safe" technology of chlorofluorocarbons. James Lovelock had shown how technology-driven deforestation could dry up the Panama Canal. Agricultural technology had stripped crop fields of their fecundity, which then had to be replaced by expensive fertilizers. Nuclear weapons technology had escalated tribal wars into global genocide. The technological way seemed to be violent, get-rich-quick, machismo-ridden, corner-cutting. It created more problems than it solved.

Even AIDS, Carl Sagan pointed out, is "partly technologically driven, because the planet has become a sexually intercommunicating whole, because of the technology of modern transportation." Had technology's maleficent influence not seeped into the ecological network of the planet, poisoning every root and leaf?

It wasn't just modern-day technology that was destructive. The rot had set in early in our history. In his talk, Sagan stepped out into space and back in time and from this far vantage point he scanned the world and its human inhabitants from the dawn of civilization to the present day.

"We started out," he said, "as hunter-gatherers, profoundly attuned to and in harmony with our environments. They formed egalitarian democracies, because the very nature of the hunter-gatherer lifestyle does not permit chiefs or social hierarchies.

Equality must be built very deeply into us, despite the anomaly of the last few thousand years."

So what went wrong? Human invention running counter to the rhythmic flow of natural life—in other words, technological intervention—complicated the issue in the form of an agricultural revolution. It consisted of an experiment with a revolutionary new idea: settling down in one spot. "Instead of wandering for great distances to find plants and game, you make a few vegetables grow nearby. Then you have a much more reliable food source, gathered with much less effort. It has not worked out that way. . . . The carrying capacity of the planet, which now contains more than five billion people, is simply inadequate for hunter-gatherer life-styles. There is no way back. . . . We have ejected ourselves from Eden and we must make do."

In other ways, too, human aspiration very early on ran counter to natural patterns.

> The kinds of malefactions that we are perfecting today go back ten thousand years or more. Eleven thousand and five hundred years ago, more or less, humans made the first large-scale crossing from Asia into North America across the Bering land bridge. This was the time of great glaciations: the ocean levels were so low that you could cross from Siberia to Alaska on dry land. Some thousand years later—about 10,500 years ago—those humans had reached Tierra del Fuego at the southernmost tip of South America. In one thousand years they had simply walked through the entire hemisphere North to South. In the process they seem to have wiped out all the large mammals that were the most characteristic aspect of that biological landscape.

So human beings have had a history of pursuing aspirations that lead us to push against the boundaries of knowledge—and in the process, to assert ourselves aggressively against our environment to the detriment of the biosphere.

Why, I wondered, have we needed to assert ourselves like this? Perhaps it was not only humans: everything alive seems to expend a huge amount of energy to stay alive as itself, and not fade back into the Earth. It seems as if there is a powerful upward force to be different, to be uniquely ourselves, in order to counter-act the huge gravitational force pulling us down into the anony-mous dust. We see it in the urge a baby has to explore and leave the mother, to counteract the desire to return to the safe anonymity of the womb. Perhaps this was what Jung talked about when he spoke of the need to individuate; perhaps this was what the Adam and Eve story was about: the need to separate from an undifferen-tiated innocence in Eden, through aspiring to self-knowledge, painful but necessary.

But this heroic, aspiring thrust towards independence—to-wards separateness and self-preservation—seems in humans to go beyond its due bounds. Individual aspiration needs to be kept in balance by wisdom and love: a man may wish to have twice as much food on his plate, but seeing his brother's hungry face will stop him from stealing his portion. If he cannot see his face, or does not acknowledge the man beside him as his brother, he may steal the plateful after all.

Technology distances the consequences of our actions: we in a rich country can steal food, more even than is healthy for us, from hungry people thousands of miles away, people unknown and unacknowledged as our brothers and sisters. Technology gives us the power to leap beyond the bounds of our wisdom and love: beyond the bounds of human morality. Joseph Weizenbaum, pro-fessor of computer science at MIT, once gave this example:

> You, colleague of many years, you are working on a machine consisting of two to the fifteenth and more microprocessors running simultaneously. With the help of such a machine one can first simulate then construct much more efficient, small, and lighter hydrogen bombs. Imagine, for a moment, you were an eyewitness at Hiroshima in 1945; you saw people stripped of their skin die. Would you want to make this happen a thou-sand times more? Would you so torture a single human being with your own hands? If you would not, regard-less of what end would be served, then you must stop your work.

The deepest impulse that lies behind technology, the longing to explore the limits of the known world, may be a noble, courageous human quality—risky, but noble. But it is essential that this impulse be governed by a moral sense that takes into account the consequences of these risks. In practice, however, the technological impulse tends to be governed not by morality but by the military. Weizenbaum again:

> Today we know with virtual certainty that every scientific and technical result will, if at all possible, be put to use in military systems. . . . The computer, together with the history of its development, is perhaps the key example. But we should also think in this connection of everything that has to do with flight, or of things atomic, of communications systems, satellites, space ships, and most of the scientific achievements of the human genius. We may then convince ourselves that in the concrete world in which we live, the burden of proof rests with those who assert that a specific new development is immune from the greed of the military.
>
> In these circumstances, scientific and technical workers cannot escape their responsibility to inquire about the end use of their work. They must then decide, once they know to what end it will be used, whether or not they would serve those ends with their own hands.

Carl Sagan told the conference: "We have acquired the kind of powers that previously were thought to be restricted to God alone. Well, with these powers comes the clear requirement for increased responsibility." But where were the signs of responsibility being taken?

The greatest danger posed by technology in the service of the military is generally regarded as the nuclear race between the U.S. and the U.S.S.R. After Sagan's passionate plea for global cooperation and de-escalation, it was particularly dramatic that the next distinguished scientist to speak that Tuesday morning should be Dr. Evguenij Velikhov, the vice president of the Soviet Academy of Sciences and a close advisor to Mikhail Gorbachev.

It was a great coup for the conference organizers to have such a senior Russian official here. Dr. Velikhov was intense, formidably frank, often humorous. Later I heard that he had arrived in the U.S. wearing a T-shirt (a top Russian official in a T-shirt?) with an antinuclear slogan on it—something like "Arms are for hugging." However true or false the T-shirt story was, at Oxford he was approachable, enthusiastically issuing an invitation to continue the work of the conference in Moscow. Dr. Velikhov focused tightly on why the technological impulse was so dangerous. The main problem was the way it pushed past the limits of our knowledge— although people talked about technological developments as though they were based on hard fact. He took Star Wars as an example.

The idea of an impenetrable shield around the world sounds good, he said, but we do not even know if it is technically possible to build such a shield in our lifetime. "This shield consists of many layers of very sophisticated weapons in space, and these weapons are connected to a very sophisticated system of communication control and measurement. Altogether they compose an extremely sophisticated system, based around the globe. How do we test this system? How do we test this system not in the theoretical but in the real environment? We have no chance to test this system. If we test this system we may not survive. In such a case we have a choice: to have knowledge, but without people, or to have people but without knowledge."

Despite this choice being manifestly absurd, building the shield is where the money and creative energy of the world could go, if certain politicians have their way: "What happens if we spend ten trillion dollars or rubles, and for this mobilized all the scientific resources of this planet, to build such an immense shield. We have no chance really to know. Is it a real shield or is it just nothing? In such a case I think, in my understanding, we have no such choice for the future. We need to follow another way, to follow another vision."

Nuclear deterrence went down no better with Dr. Velikhov than with Carl Sagan. Again, he pointed out, we were putting our trust in systems that went far beyond our knowledge and control— and even beyond common sense.

"The idea of deterrence is based on two assumptions: the assumption of credibility and the assumption of internal safety. But these two contradict each other. If you wish to increase the credibility . . . you immediately decrease the safety, because we shorten the fuse, shorten the time between the first launch and the decision to retaliate. Increase the power of the weapons and you push the opponent into a much more difficult position—into a position of possible decision to launch on warning or other measures, which of course decreases the general stability."

Our so-called security through deterrence is not based on sound scientific argument at all—it is based on a hopeless fallacy. Nuclear deterrence does not remove the danger of nuclear war, it merely bullies the warring parties into a precarious and sullen silence—to be ended any moment by a terrible explosion: "Such a solution [is like] putting a ten-ton high explosive with a very short fuse in your kitchen to solve family quarrels."

To many critics, he said, the idea of weapons for deterrence is illogical. "But for many political thinkers, many political leaders, and military specialists today, the idea of deterrence is sound and in some way moral. Some people argue, after forty-three years of peace in Europe, the longest period of peace, that nuclear weapons are the main reason why we have peace today. But I think in this case we go into another problem of the problem."

The "problem of the problem" arises because our knowledge is limited, though we push against its limits as though it were secure. Dr. Velikhov asked, How can our knowledge be secure? If we have a hypothesis about the structure of the atom, we can conduct tests to prove it true or false. But how can we prove the efficacy of defence systems that cannot, by definition, be tested in reality? How many Earths can we destroy in tests? We must learn to recognize our limits: that was his emphatically repeated message.

We are not inclined to acknowledge limits; on the contrary, we tend to regard as heroic the people who press hardest against limits—whether they climb the highest mountain or run a mile faster than ever before. An illuminating TV investigation on why people build skyscrapers suggested that architects' talk of building high for reasons of economy was not the whole story—that they were really vying to be the ones who built the tallest erections.

High performance has been a matter of breaking records, being taller, bigger, faster. Other, subtler, criteria of quality rarely count. A cow race witnessed by the poet P. J. Cavanagh on a remote tropical island must be an exception. The cow that won wasn't the fastest—it was the one that moved most gracefully.

Carl Sagan, too, had despaired in his talk of our macho competitiveness. "If we must compete, can't we have an honesty race?" he had asked exasperatedly. Would humankind ever be prepared to slow down and think, to look before it leapt—or would it always leap arrogantly first and regret later?

Dr. Velikhov gave us a rare and cheering example of a politician looking first. There was a proposal, he said, to irrigate the south of the Soviet Union by reversing the Siberian rivers. But the government stopped the process, not because opponents of the scheme gave evidence of adverse effects, but because they realized that they simply did not know what would happen after such a big change in the environment. They didn't assume the scheme was innocent until proven guilty; they knew that they didn't know—and that was argument enough to hold back.

When it comes to nuclear deterrence strategy, however, the people in charge prefer to push aside their knowledge that they don't know. "The problem," said Dr. Velikhov, "is that we do not know exactly how it works. We have no real theory, and we have no specialists. For such big things, it is impossible to have real knowledge. For real knowledge we need experiments. We need another Earth—maybe not one, maybe thousands of Earths—to make such experiments. In such cases, I think we need to understand the limit of our knowledge." Yet we continue to take huge risks.

"If some extraterrestrial creatures visited us today," he had said, when he introduced the idea of the balance of terror, "after examining our culture, our intelligence, they would be very surprised at the terrible nuclear situation we have on Earth." He described the strategy of "mutually assured destruction" as "maybe not strategy but reality."

The conference had heard two top scientists, one from each of the two superpowers, denouncing each in his own way the manifestation of human ingenuity and aspiration in the form of nuclear weapons. What most interested me in what Dr. Velikhov was saying was his point about knowledge. The credibility of science—even the very word—is based on its being grounded in knowledge. Scientists and other hard-nosed professionals, such as politicians, were supposed to base their actions on secure factual knowledge—unlike spiritual leaders or artists, who were willing to launch into the realms of faith and mystery. And yet here we were being told clearly that the most dangerous and expensive weapons the world has ever known were being devised on a basis of insufficient real knowledge. Perhaps it is truer to say that scientific adventurers, no less than other adventurers into unknown territory, trespass beyond knowledge into mystery, and because they do, they need to take with them as much wisdom, care, and reverence as do those who deal in the realms of imagination and the spirit.

How could scientists better occupy themselves than with building nuclear weapons? They could use their ingenuity to de-escalate the arms race, instead of using it to escalate it further. Their first step should be to dismantle the old vision. "How do we build the next century without nuclear weapons?" Dr. Velikhov was prepared to go much further than the INF treaty which proposed reducing the nuclear arsenal by 50 percent. The world might be impressed by this figure but he was not. He "did not see any problem in using realistic means of verification to go down to 5 percent of the arsenals we have today. . . . It is necessary to step from confrontation to cooperation, because it is in the interests of all countries around the globe to build a real, verifiable environment in which it is possible to go down to a very low level [of nuclear weapons]—to a final goal of a nonnuclear world."

But wasn't verification an impossibility? Dr. Velikhov didn't think so, not if the matter were left to scientists. They were the real verification experts, he believed, not professional negotiators: "For thirty years the 'experts' have discussed this problem. . . . But in May of 1986 the American scientists from the National Resource Defense Counsel approached us at the Academy of Science, and asked for cooperation to really study the problem of verification of very small explosions. Never in my life has it happened so fast. In May we had discussions. In June we had an agreement." The verification experiment was conducted in July in the U.S.S.R., the Russian scientists cooperating with American scientists. Shortly after the conference Dr. Velikhov visited test sites in Nevada with other Soviet scientists. (Presumably it was on this visit that he wore the T-shirt).

He was very enthusiastic about the future of scientific cooperation. "I am very grateful," he said, "for support from great American foundations, MacArthur, Carnegie, Rockefeller and others, because they made this experiment possible. After similar experiments, we agreed to organize the new international foundation for the survival and development of mankind. It was organized in Moscow this February [1988]. Not only is verification important. The building of trust is important. The building of trust is again a cooperative measure."

He ended his speech with a brief discussion of nuclear energy. Referring to Sagan's arguments about carbon dioxide contamination and the viability of nuclear energy, he offered his belief that some form of nuclear energy might be possible. But he was concerned with safety. He didn't believe that the nuclear reactors we had now were safe in the long term: "It is a shame we have not spent enough money and resources to cooperate together for safe nuclear power." As Chernobyl was on everyone's mind, he said ironically: "From the point of view of military significance, Chernobyl was not an explosion at all!"

Not just nuclear war but any war could release nuclear radiation. Dr. Velikhov reminded us that power plants are highly vulnerable targets during a war: "A fire in highly industrialized countries," he said, "is highly dangerous. . . . In any development for the future, we need to move to a completely different world without war."

As for nuclear fusion as a source of power, there "we have had twenty-five years of cooperation," and he had faith in the fusion reactor that had just begun to be built by a Soviet-American-Japanese-European team. Cooperation in the field of nuclear energy, he said, "is our chance and our hope."

Neither Dr. Velikhov nor Carl Sagan labeled modern technology—even nuclear technology—as intrinsically good or evil. The question was, rather, whether it existed in the service of aggression or in a context of cooperation. The idea was not to do away with technology, nor the impulse to press against the limits of knowledge that lies at the heart of science, but to do away with war and warlike competitiveness, for these are wasteful of human talent and the world's wealth—even when they are not actively deployed in mass destruction. Technology is the application of science. How and why it is applied is a matter of human values, though it

51

seemed to me that there is a built-in weighting on the side of risk and danger.

Carl Sagan said, "The common enemy is not so much other nations as the misuse of technology and the dangers that our own aggressive instincts pose to ourselves." But how can we ever ensure that technology will not be misused, if it remains vulnerable to abuse until we surrender our aggressive instincts? When will humans surrender their aggressive instincts forever? At least not until we recognize that, quite literally, there is no future in war. Until then, as Professor Weizenbaum of MIT said, "in the concrete world in which we live, the burden of proof rests with those who assert that a specific new development is immune from the greed of the military."

Barbara Marx Hubbard, one of the conference participants and a tireless networker for new values, believed that "the next big shift will be on war. War will not be considered legitimate—at all. It will be delegitimized." The antipathy to war was echoed by Manuel Ulloa, former prime minister of Peru. "Power and wealth tend to be selfish and want to perpetuate themselves, obviously at the expense of others less fortunate," he said, adding unequivocally: "They administer the diabolical arms industry that legalizes murder."

I found this characterization of war as "legalized murder" immensely empowering. To see war as nebulously powerful and frightening, like an unpredictable monster, is disempowering; to see it as an illicit act deliberately performed by certain men and women—illicit morally if not yet juridically—reminds us that war is not beyond our control. As an act chosen by people, it is amenable to change by people.

As a society, we have decided now that we do not approve of acts where one person imposes their will on another to the point of extinguishing the other's life. When we hear of such acts we call them murders, and we search the murderers out and imprison them for their cruel and antisocial behavior. Until we perceive warmongers similarly, we will not treat them as criminals. Instead we will continue to vote them into office as our leaders, and offer them our hard-earned money to pay for weapons of destruction— weapons of mass murder.

Dr. Weizenbaum had said of our defense weapons: "Those

aren't weapons, they are mass murder machines and mass murder machine delivery systems. That is how we should speak of them: clearly, distinctly, and without evasion. Once we recognize that a nuclear mass murder machine is nothing other than an instant Auschwitz—without railroads or Eichmanns or Dr. Mengele, but an Auschwitz just the same—can we continue then to work on systems that steer these devices to living cities?"

A better attitude to war than ours was expressed by a Quaker to Voltaire in 1733. He was so impressed that he repeated it, untranslated, in *Letters concerning the English Nation:*

> We never war or fight in any case; but it is not that we are afraid, for so far from shuddering at the thoughts of death, we on the contrary bless the moment which unites us with the Being of Beings; but the reason of our not using the outward sword is, that we are neither wolves, tigers, not mastiffs, but men and Christians.
>
> Our God, who has commanded us to love our enemies, and to suffer without repining, would certainly not permit us to cross the seas, merely because murderers clothed in scarlet, and wearing caps two foot high, enlist citizens by a noise made with two little sticks on an ass's skin extended.
>
> And when, after a victory is gained, the whole city of London is illuminated; when the sky is in a blaze with fireworks, and a noise is heard in the air, of thanksgivings, of bells, of organs, and of the cannon, we groan in silence, and are deeply affected with sadness of spirit and brokenness of heart, for the sad havoc which is the occasion of those public rejoicings.

5 *Planetary Therapy*

> Man made the aeroplane and the Ape got hold
> of it.
>
> H. G. WELLS

THE hydra had been found. Environmental breakdown, nuclear violence, mass poverty—all these dangers were found to have a common source, and it lay in the psyche of the human being.

We could no longer blame a baleful Nature or acts of a vengeful God for the problems of global survival. It was human egotism, insecurity, and greed that were wrecking the planet. These negative forces are not the only inner qualities a human possesses, but they seem recently to have taken the upper hand. Could our other, more positive qualities be released in time to save us and our planet? Or are we caught in a culture that fosters our negativity?

Father Tom Berry was in no doubt about the effect of our technology-driven culture:

> The industrial world is a kind of entrancement, a pathology. It's addictive. We become addicted to automobiles. It's paralyzing, because once we're totally caught up in it, we think we can't do anything about it. We have a type of religious commitment to the industrial world. And that's the difficulty now: these new movements to strengthen the corporative enterprise by what they call "humanizing" it are giving it a human mission, a mythic dimension. All their advertising goes deep into the deepest motivations of the human psychic sense; they use children, the home, religious festivals, everything is used—but that moves us from disaster to disaster, because the process itself is pathological, suicidal.

I wondered about the use of the hero image in advertising. Berry agreed:

Particularly that. The mythic Paradise—it's offering Wonderworld. But we don't get Wonderworld, we get Wasteworld. We're trashing the wonderful, ever-renewing natural systems in order to produce—junk! It's so ridiculous. Look at automobile advertising. It's hysterical. It's like a drug. I think the automobile has become the central reality of American civilization. Children can't go to college any more without a car.

There are now four hundred million automobiles. In the U.S., there's one for every 1.8 persons. In China, there's one for every twenty-three-thousand! We will have to go through the withdrawal processes we associate with drug addiction.

And we wonder why religious people are so insensitive to this, why they are so accepting about it. They really have not the slightest idea what's happening.

Might it be, I asked, because many of the religious people who live in the industrial world lead relatively sheltered and affluent lives? They live among the dreamy benefits of the industrial system, not the debris.

"Even for them the dream is only temporary," said Father Berry.

Because the pollution is reaching into the beaches, into the summer homes; even they are progressively being disturbed, their dream world is being sullied. It has hit people at what they like most—they dream of going to the seashore, but there they find themselves in junk: "I'm swimming in garbage."

Take the candidates for the U.S. presidency—every once in a while they mention ecology. They didn't mention ecology in politics until the trash showed up, though it's known for a long time. . . .

"Progress" is the central word of modern civilization. It's the central word of the industrial order—an order that did not come through spiritual means. In the seventeenth century the Western world decided, "We'll do it with technology, with science. We'll do it by taking control of the natural world, we'll make the natural

55

world yield up its abundance for our use; we're going
to create Wonderworld."

But what could make us change if we are so hooked? This was the
key question of the conference. We had spent the first part of it
analyzing the problem. If the heart of the hydra was a deep
pathology in humans and their present culture, then the single
most important question for our survival is; What could change
that? Tom Berry had a stark first answer:

> Terror! Something has to crash. The really depress-
> ing thing about this period is that we will take so many
> things down with us. We'll take the rain forests. Every
> minute of every day, we're losing fifty acres of rain
> forest. Every minute of every day, fifty acres, forever
> . . . for the rain forest will not come back. It's irreversi-
> ble.

> The future of our children is going to be terribly
> deprived. We're losing ten thousand species every year.
> So far we have only recorded the existence of a million
> and a half species, though there are more. We're going
> to lose perhaps a million species. And many of the
> species we lose will be among the most brilliant—spe-
> cies from the insect world, without which nothing else
> functions; they will be small life forms, like plankton in
> the sea, that make the oxygen in the air. Without these
> species, nothing functions.

> The industrial world is just too devastating to en-
> dure. To deal with economics: we talk about the corpo-
> ration deficit, the national deficit, the trade deficit, the
> Third World interest deficit. Nobody talks about Earth
> deficit.

> Economics is a religious issue. Recently a group of
> bishops in the U.S. were asking that everybody be
> incorporated into the functioning of our economic sys-
> tem and into its benefits—that's the general social ap-
> proach, that everybody needs a job; you get a job and
> with the job you make money and with money you
> participate in the process.

> But what if the process is disastrous? And the jobs
> in it are disastrous—because the jobs are doing things

that should not be done. People say a job is a job and you get a salary. But if you put people to work cutting down all the forests, building dams and spreading poisons all over the place—that's a job. You can pay a person for that. But what's happening? How long can it last? The sense of this is like drug addiction again.

A short-term fix tends to be seen even by socially concerned leaders as "the solution"—instead of seeing the long-term consequences of these myopic fixes. Father Berry continued:

I'm trying to get religious people to appreciate the order of magnitude of the change that is taking place. I find consistently that people underestimate what's happening because what's happening now has no historical parallel, no biological parallel, for the changes that the industrial system has brought about on the planet. We're changing the chemistry of the planet on the scale of hundreds of millions of years. We're changing the biosystems of the planet on a similar scale. We're even changing the geology of the planet.

These are things that we never even thought of before. And the way in which these changes are taking place did not happen even in prior times when there were great species extinctions and great changes, at the end of the Paleozoic era, 225 million years ago, or at the end of the Mesozoic era, sixty-five million years ago. The very structure of the planet is changing.

A lot of people approach what's happening as though it were narrowly about political or economic issues, but it is just enormously more than that; and if we do not attend to the larger dimensions of things, then none of our social programs have much chance of succeeding.

I always think of this cartoon I saw once. Somebody fell off the Empire State Building. As he's passing the thirty-fourth floor, he waves at the guy in the window and says, "I'm doing great so far!"

Yes . . . we're doing great so far.

If the industrial process is a manifestation of cultural pathology, what is the way out? Father Berry gave his second and more surprising answer: "We need a deep cultural therapy."

Therapy for a stricken planet. Planetary therapy. Once I'd gotten over the surprise, it seemed to me a sensible answer. The source of our problems lay, after all, inside ourselves. An inner healing was what we needed, so that we could dare to operate from our better inner impulses instead of our most negative ones. At present, we hid our best qualities and proffered our worst: we displayed our tawdry wealth, we made frightening faces at our enemies, we flexed our muscles like Mr. Universe—and we hid, because they were too tender and precious to show to a dangerous world, our qualities of goodness and truthfulness, our vulnerable hearts and our sublime possibilities.

Shakespeare had said it in *Measure for Measure*:

> Man, proud man,
> Dressed in a little brief authority,
> Most ignorant of what he's most assured,
> His glassy essence, like an angry ape,
> Plays such fantastic tricks before high heaven
> As makes the angels weep.

We had been behaving like the angry ape for too many centuries, pitting our puny strength against the discreet might of Gaia. The more we showed off, the more we revealed our foolishness—and the more we guaranteed our self-destruction. We were still caught in petty clannishness, as Sagan had shown, and in grand larceny, as the environmentalists had shown. We were insecure—clinging to the badges of our tribe, constantly making our tribe better and more righteous than any other to prop up any niggling internal doubts. We were greedy, feeding our egos with property, which in turn bolstered the myth of our grandeur and our right to dominate anyone less wealthy than ourselves. And above all we were unhappy, cut off and confused about meaning: was there meaning in life, and did we have a valid place in that meaning?

We needed now to soothe our angry ape and make him take note that his true security lies not in reckless displays of outer, physical power but in the quiet realm of his glassy essence. That is where meaning and purpose reside.

During my own training as a therapist, I had observed many psychotherapy sessions where people underwent a profound inner healing. The sessions were very moving; the observers often watched with tears coursing down their cheeks. Patients would come into the therapy room feeling trapped in a hostile world, full of fear and jealousy, either angry and frustrated or their energy deadened with impotent rage.

But sometimes, perhaps after many months of work, perhaps in the very first meeting, something mysterious would happen in the interchange between patient and therapist—and an ancient trap would spring open. The patients would be free of an old, unconscious bind; they would be able to move and breathe again. They would begin to be who they really were—not who they imagined they ought to be. Those of us who had observed a sad and angry ape tearing at iron bars now silently welcomed a more complete human being stepping into life.

What were the features of this process of empowerment? Could it happen outside the individual therapy room, on a planetary level? Could it happen here, at the conference—which was, after all, a microcosm of the planet, with representatives from its many tribal groups? In what ways, I asked myself, could this conference act as a planetary therapy section?

The first and most obvious feature of a therapy session, I recalled, was talking. The patient did a lot of talking. Well, there was no shortage of talking at Oxford, no more than at any conference.

A second and less obvious feature was listening—the therapist, especially, did a lot of high quality listening. At Oxford, despite the conferees being representatives of groups that were embattled in the outside world, there was a remarkable amount of listening—uncontentious, genuinely interested listening—unlike most conferences, where people usually bide their time when others are speaking, hoping they will hurry up and finish so they can push their own point of view.

A third feature was the willingness to let go, bit by bit, of those mind-sets that have been ground into our psyches in the past. And an essential fourth feature, in the sessions that worked, was caring. Often the therapy room was the first place where a person had ever experienced the certainty of being loved. The shock of this feeling of love was, in my experience, sometimes overwhelming; it would release sobs that sounded more like agony than joy—and indeed were, first of all, an expression of agony, for the oldest wound had been touched, the deepest longing of any human being: to be utterly loved.

I had heard spiritual leaders talk readily of love. But they seemed to talk mostly about giving love. Even when you felt starved of love yourself, they asked you to scrape the bottom of the barrel and find more love, more energy, to give out to others. It seemed an exhausting business—and rarely appeared to change anything. How could ordering someone to love possibly help? Tell a sweatshop employer he should love his workers? Tell a cruel teacher to love his pupils? Or even try telling an unconfident person that they should love themselves more? The answer would almost certainly be, "I know I should—but how can I if I don't?" Exactly. How can they? So how were we to help these angry apes who don't love other people, or the Earth, or themselves?

Worse, most of the people who talked most glibly of love and loving others seemed to me the most coldly (and unconsciously) judgmental in practice. They wanted so much to be on the side of love that they denied the existence of all their "lesser" feelings— their envy, their anger, their hurt, their vengefulness—and projected these feelings onto everyone else. The result was that they came over as saccharine and false; and they read into the people around them all the bitterness that they denied in themselves. They didn't see the people standing before them; they saw only their denied feelings reflected and didn't know it. So when they were angry with you, they imagined that they were peaceful and you were angry; when they were frightened like a child, they criticized you for being childish and afraid.

The difference between all this and love in the therapy room was that patients weren't lectured about giving love; they began with the experience of being loved, receiving an experience of their own lovability. Only then did patients have the chance of awakening their own inner spring of love and having some, at last, to give.

But could this experience be replicated on a global level? And, anyway, how far could an individual feeling better about himself or herself really change what was happening on the planet? We had at the conference the most celebrated apostle of love alive: Mother Teresa of Calcutta. She was due to speak the following day. Perhaps she would enlighten us.

6 *Life in the Shadows*

Love bade one welcome; yet my soul drew back,
Guilty of dust and sin.

GEORGE HERBERT

MOTHER Teresa is held high in public esteem as a kind of universal saint, transcending national and denominational boundaries. Although she is a Catholic, even anti-Catholics melt in admiration at her name. Although she is Albanian, few people know or care about her national origin. She blithely ignores the sensitivities of patriots who will not tolerate their country being criticized in any way by an 'outsider'—and gets away with it. When Mother Teresa says that she has met people in London living in cardboard boxes "like coffins," who are worse off than the poor in the Third World, Mrs. Thatcher hurries to be photographed being kind to her.

Mother Teresa is seen as a saint of the people, and especially of the poorest people. Those whom we, the well-heeled, classify as "outside society" she draws in within her wide circle of acceptance. And, most unusual of all in a modern world where productivity is the highest value, she offers her energy to the dying—those whom a mercantilist society inevitably accounts the most irrelevant, since they create no wealth.

Mother Teresa was scheduled to make a statement midweek. But she had already intervened unexpectedly by asking Dean Morton to read aloud a prayer at the opening of the conference. On every seat there had been placed a folded piece of paper with a grainy photocopy on the front of Mother Teresa holding a small boy in her arms. We had unfolded the small sheets to find this Prayer for Peace:

> Make us worthy, Lord,
> to serve our fellow men throughout the world
> who live and die in poverty and hunger.

> Give them, through our hands, this day their daily
>   bread;
> and by our understanding love, give peace and joy.
>
> Lord, make me a channel of Thy peace, that,
> where there is hatred, I may bring love;
> where there is wrong, I may bring the spirit of
>   forgiveness;
> where there is discord, I may bring harmony;
> where there is error, I may bring truth;
> where there is doubt, I may bring faith;
> where there is despair, I may bring hope;
> where there are shadows, I may bring light;
> where there is sadness, I may bring joy.
>
> Lord, grant that I may seek rather to comfort
> than to be comforted,
> to understand than to be understood;
> to love than to be loved;
> for it is by forgetting self that one finds oneself;
> it is by forgiving that one is forgiven;
> it is by dying that one awakens to eternal life.
> Amen.

It was a powerful gesture, linking us at once to the people at the margins of society that most of us would rather forget about. I found it impossible to say the words other than sincerely, and to do that was to make an uncompromising commitment to love—a love that stretched all the way from our comfortable home bases to the ragged margins of society.

And it was a daring gesture, unexpectedly asking a multifaith conference to say a Christian prayer together. But we did—and, as far as I know, without a murmur of dissent: Jewish rabbi beside Buddhist monk, Hindu pilgrim beside atheist scientist; whatever the particular color of our beliefs, everyone in the hall made a commitment in unison to act with the generosity of love.

One thing worried me, though, about Mother Teresa's prayer. "It is by forgetting self that one finds oneself" sounded uncomfortably sacrificial for my taste—too martyrish. Should the circles of sympathy be expanded by "forgetting self" or by "adding to self"?

This tendency to selflessness was one of the things that worried me about spiritual leaders. I felt I had only just "found myself," after many years of struggle; that was true, too, for many of my friends. Learning to love ourselves and not feel unlovable, unworthy, all the time—that had been a hard task for most of us. Were we supposed to sacrifice all that again? I decided I would try to find an opportunity to speak to Mother Teresa later on and ask her directly.

Midweek, Mother Teresa made her scheduled speech. Instead of standing at the podium, she knelt behind it and delivered her entire speech on her knees. Her speech, unexpectedly, was not warm; or at any rate, I did not find it so.

She spoke of the poor, vividly, but I had the uncomfortable feeling of being manipulated by a practiced rhetorician. "The family that prays together stays together, and if you stay together you will love one another as God loves you in a tender love," she said.

> The tenderness of God's love is so beautiful. I experience that so often in our homes for the dying. Last night also, those people, they opened their little boxes made of cardboard. They were inside that cardboard, made like a little coffin. I simply didn't know what to say. My eyes were full of tears. These people, lying in the cardboard protecting themselves from the cold, and the joy they felt just because somebody could smile at them, who could be concerned for them. It changed something. This little act of love brought a beautiful smile onto their faces.
>
> You and I have gathered here together not to discuss big things and small, but to find out, to bring back love in our families, to bring peace and joy in our families, to bring prayer back again into our families. The family that prays together stays together.

My anxiety was heightened sharply when she launched into polemic, denouncing abortion and the use of contraception:

> We are afraid for ourselves but we are not afraid for the millions of children that are being killed. I cannot

remember now who said that every second so many little ones are being aborted. . . . We in our mission are fighting abortion by adoption. We see how those little ones have brought so much joy into homes where the family cannot have a child. I never give a child to a family that has used contraceptives to not have a child, because using contraceptives kills the power of loving, kills the power of being loved. Therefore, how can a mother love a child of somebody if she has killed the joy of loving. This is something that we must all take to heart.

Natural family planning is something very beautiful, very simple. We are teaching it to our leper families, to our beggars, to our street people. Many of these people have come to thank me for allowing the sisters to teach them. They say that "from the time you have taught us, our families have remained healthy. We are close to each other and we can have a baby whenever we want."

I found her talk quite frightening—especially when she said, "I never give a child to a family that has used contraceptives to not have a child." Was there anyone in the audience (married, or in a similar relationship) who had never used a contraceptive? Were so many of us condemned out of hand as "killers of love"? Surely we used contraceptives to guard those we loved.

Her statistic, for example ("I cannot remember now who said that every second so many little ones are being aborted"), was wildly inapposite: it proved the opposite of what she had used it to prove. No one had said "so many children are being aborted every second". On the contrary, the calculation, which had been cited by Jim Grant of UNICEF earlier in the conference, had referred to children who had died, pitifully, after their birth, because their parents were too poor to keep them alive. Was this death, after the struggle to be born, better than nonconception? Could adoption possibly solve a problem of this magnitude?

What was a mother to do who found herself pregnant yet again, when she hadn't the money or the energy to feed the children to whom she had already given birth? She might choose

65

an abortion rather than watch her already living children die from lack of food and care. Surely it would be better for her to use contraception, so she does not need to find herself in this dreadful predicament in the future.

A child dies every other second because of poverty. These are children with names and loved faces, who die in the slow agony of hunger and disease. Which of us has not seen, on TV if we are rich, or with our own eyes if we live among the poor, the too-brilliant eyes of a child dying of poverty, with flies in her face that she is too weak to brush away?

Fred Sai, the Ghanaian population advisor to the World Bank, had spoken to the conference just before Mother Teresa. He had been passionate about the violence done to women and children—not just the violence of physical and verbal attack in scenes of domestic violence, but the violence of constant pregnancy and childbirth. Girls who became mothers too young had little chance of becoming people in their own right. (I remembered a poster that urged wisely: "Before you be a mother, be a woman.") Young women who were pregnant again and again, with little choice in the matter, became weak and prematurely old. Their babies, too, were weak, far more likely to die than babies born to women who spaced their pregnancies out, and who didn't start to have children until they had finished their education.

We should take to heart the evidence about the biggest single factor helping the fight against infant mortality. It is not social class, or income, or the age of the mother. It is, astonishingly, the *education* of the mother. Why should this be so? The answer seems to be that the more educated the mother, the more confident she is—the more empowered. She feels able to trust her own instincts and feels less pushed around by the guilt and anxiety instilled by other members of her family or social group. It is the babies of clear-headed women like this who tend to survive and flourish; it is not literacy per se but the confidence that comes with it that extends the power of the young mother and of her baby to live.

Were we now to tell these women to return to guilt and self-abnegation—submitting passively to a life of constant childbearing, leading to premature death for themselves and for their children?

Fred Sai had been orphaned and brought up motherlessly in an institution. He had balanced the value of the unborn child with the value of the mother and the born child. "Mere survival," he said, "is not enough." It was inhuman to be an unwanted child these days, when it was no longer necessary.

Hanna Klaus, another participant, said that although she too disapproved of artificial contraception, she would not insist on women abandoning it. She would merely teach them how to use natural methods of contraception and let them make their own choice. Many women participants were angry at Mother Teresa's unexpected attack on users of contraception and abortion; especially vocal were some from Latin America.

Other participants also showed their discomfort. One man who believed abortion was morally wrong nonetheless showed his distress at Mother Theresa's cold dismissal of women who, because of the terrible difficulties in their lives, had felt driven to resort to it. One woman said she thought Mother Teresa was dangerous, and being used by people less naive then herself.

A spiritual leader who had once been a parliamentary leader— and could never be accused of naiveté—saw how troubled I was by all this and drew me aside into a corridor. What was the matter? he asked.

I wanted to know if he thought Mother Teresa was an exemplar of how to be truly loving. She had helped me with her words that day and had inspired many others for years. She talked of love constantly and she seemed to equate love with being a guardian of life. All that was fine, I said. Of course we should be guardians of life rather than dealers of death.

But life wasn't always lived under ideal circumstances. Women weren't always married to men who would acquiesce in natural methods of contraception. Maybe the poverty-stricken men to whom Mother Teresa gave her personal attention were willing to be educated, but most women I knew had their sexual wishes laughed at by their husbands, or simply ignored, and they couldn't wheel Mother Teresa with her powers of persuasion into their bedroom. As for the women from the poorest slums who suffered miserable abortions or were grateful for any contraception—surely they were the people who gave the most to their families and received the least support in the world? Weren't they the women who deserved most to be loved, not rejected as killers of love? Was

67

Mother Teresa a saint of love, or a very human, dogmatic, bossy old woman?

"Of course she is a saint," he said. "But she is a saint toward her constituency, which is a very particular one; this constituency—of the destitute and dying—may cross certain boundaries, but it is still very narrow. About other things, she doesn't know. And perhaps she doesn't want to know. She is not a thinker; she is focused on one thing."

A one-note saint. That made sense. If Mother Teresa identified love with bringing out into the light and caring for the hidden life of the unwanted, then she would of course focus on the life beating vestigially in the dying destitute, hidden in the shadows of dark streets, and on the life beating in the heart of the unborn child, hidden in the womb, or even in the child, still more invisible, who might have been born, had not contraception intervened. Someone, presumably, had to stand up for the invisible and unwanted human, and it was Mother Teresa who played that part, just as James Lovelock had announced himself as standing for the parts of nature that no one else cared for.

What Mother Teresa was doing, then, was not standing for the whole, not standing for universal love, but adding one essential piece to a picture; the piece of the multicolored jigsaw of love that had fallen under the table. As some women become—justifiably—clearer about guarding their right to be respected and cared for, and the right of their existing children to be respected and cared for, of course there must arise others like Mother Theresa who remind us of the consequent sacrifice: all the children who might have been born.

Think of the children that Mother Teresa herself might have borne, had she not chosen to be a nun. There are always sacrifices. A problem arose only if we tried to decide which of the two sides was totally right; which side totally represents love, and which is totally banishable as representing sacrifice. As far as I could understand, both sides represented love—and both represented sacrifice.

After her speech a press conference was going to be held, and I saw that now was my chance to ask her my question about selflessness and sacrifice. We sat beside a window in the mayor's room, she and I, and whispered together, our heads bent, as the pressmen and women jostled into place.

I asked her my question. Do we not need to learn to love ourselves, to learn that we are lovable, before we can love others? It is a difficult process for many of us.

She seemed surprised that valuing myself was a problem. She replied with simple certainty; "But you are precious to God."

Something happened for me in that moment. It was as if the walls fell open. I was overwhelmed by a feeling of being loved, of being indeed valuable, precious to life itself. In the distance—in fact, very close to me—I heard her words continue, less clearly. She was saying something about God's love for all his creation, but I barely heard. Of course, I wanted to say, of course; how could I have been so stupid? It was as though I had been searching everywhere with my head down, when I only needed to look up. And then the moment passed, and I was back in a crowded room. There were reporters pressing. I remembered my list of questions and stumbled through them, holding my tape recorder as close as I could to our faces. In fact, the room was so noisy, I could hardly make out a word on the tape. In any case, nothing that we said after that did more than give me time to come back to Earth.

I stayed on for part of the press conference, but the questions asked seemed irrelevant. Why ask Mother Theresa if there were more poor people in London now or before? She couldn't possibly know. She wasn't a social statistician. She was being fed cues, obviously, to make her say controversial lines, to make one place better or worse, one time better or worse, than another. Divisions, comparisons—they made good copy but they were utterly beside the point for someone who stood for inclusivity, not for quantifying and defining. I could hear her say, defensively, "I never compare."

Information wasn't her forte. Politics wasn't her field. Numbering wasn't her game. Quality, not quantity, was the issue here. What she was good at was being sure that life was precious—everyone's life, even mine, though I was a stranger to her. The gift of that certainty had reminded me for a moment that I didn't need to justify my existence; I was justified in existing simply because I was alive. My life was part of creation. I had a place in the cosmos.

69

For a stunning moment I had been let off the hook on which I impaled myself. Like the patients in the sessions I had observed in the past, I too now had an experience of being utterly loved. I returned to Christ Church College ridiculously happy.

7 The Right to Be Heard

> Well, I don't suppose any of us is fool enough
> to think that we can save the world. But if each of
> us were to look at some of the directions we'd like
> to see the world go in, and then put one little bit
> of force behind one of them, and to have a hell of
> a good time while we're doing it, well then, that's
> what we should like to do.
>
> BILL MCLARNEY

THERE was a romantic fever in the hall when it was known that His Holiness the Dalai Lama was about to appear. Captivated by the archetypal myths that surround him—the baby magically found by wise men searching far and wide (not so different from the story that accompanies the birth of another well-known prophet), now a great leader exiled in the wilderness—the audience seemed ready to be devotees before he said a word. One young photographer whose hand he patted was so overcome she burst into tears.

Fortunately His Holiness didn't indulge in mystical manners. He chuckled a lot, very infectiously and often at his own jokes, slapped people vigorously on the arm, and waved greetings to friendly faces. As he made his slow progress up the aisle, jammed tight in a tourniquet of fans and security people, he seemed to me the sort of uncle who is a terrific guest at a family party, perking everyone up and jollying tired children out of bad humor.

On the platform, I could see him clearly at last. I was surprised at how tall he was, and how deep and singsong his voice. He addressed the conference affectionately as "brothers and sisters" and was charmingly humble. He offered, as he put it, "broken thoughts in broken English" about the importance of simple, warm feelings. All human history, the whole of human development, he said, was based on our need for these warm feelings. No matter how much material systems develop, this need will never change, so there was no point neglecting this need for warmth.

"New things," he said, "should be connected with this feeling. Science, engineering, law, politics. They are all different fingers—linked with one palm." The metaphor, though so simple, was potent. It contained a crucial theme of the conference—that of simultaneous diversity and unity. Each finger is different and has a separate identity at its own level, but all are united at the level of the palm. We had come across this dual-level concept before in political terms, when we realized that we did not need to stop belonging to our nation in order to become planetarists. Now the same principle of "the cherished whole that cherishes the part" had been applied again. When His Holiness was questioned later about this paradox of unity and diversity he applied it to yet another situation: each member of a family is a unique individual, and yet also belongs to a family.

E. F. Schumacher, author of *Small Is Beautiful,* had understood this well:

> All subjects, no matter how specialized, are connected with a center; they are like rays emanating from a sun. The center is constituted by our most basic convictions, by those ideas which really have the power to move us. In other words, the center consists of metaphysics and ethics, of ideas that—whether we like it or not—transcend the world of facts.
>
> Because they transcend the world of facts, they cannot be proved or disproved by ordinary scientific method. But that does not mean that they are purely "subjective" or "relative" or mere arbitrary conventions. They must be true to reality, although they transcend the world of facts—an apparent paradox to our positivistic thinkers. If they are not true to reality, the adherence to such a set of ideas must inevitably lead to disaster.

And what is the palm, the connecting whole, in terms of human values? "Look at your own experience," urged the Dalai Lama, his voice rising. "No need of philosophy to prove these things! Other people also need love and compassion." So we were back with love as the deepest human need and the greatest human connector. Said His Holiness, if you really want to be a successful human being, you need friends. We need human companions, because we are social animals. "But our friends may be unreliable—friends of our money or power, not friends of our being. To develop true friendship the only proper method is love and sincerity and openness."

As for economics, he said, everything is interdependent now. So "for one to improve, everyone must." And as for the environment, he cried out: "You have to care! Sometimes moral teaching, ethics, seem like a luxury. But nowadays it is not a luxury. It is a matter of survival."

The same thoughts that the other speakers had so far explained and proven in their own ways—complex, scientific, poetic—the Dalai Lama expressed so simply that a child could understand them. The future depended on the present, he said, so we were responsible now for the whole of the next generation. There was no place to hide from our problems. Except—and here he grinned—"I may survive—in small foothills of the Himalayas!" Everyone laughed. The warmth in the auditorium was tangible.

We need to realize, he said, the oneness of all human beings. "Lovingkindness is the universal religion. Even if you survive, your mental function might not be proper [without it]. Without human affectionate quality, [we] can create unpleasant experiences. In order to develop [a] healthy human society, [we] need more harmony. . . . We need [a] sense of brotherhood and sisterhood."

But what about the different religions? "Various religions have special roles," said His Holiness, "but every religion emphasizes forgiveness, tolerance, brotherhood, and sisterhood." We must "develop genuine mutual respect. Not try to propagate one's own faith, but ask 'how much can I contribute to humanity?' " Our pride in the specialness of our own religion, our faith in its special virtue, was no longer something to shelter from others, nor to impose on others, but a gift we were able to offer to the general good: fruit for the feast.

The Dalai Lama returned to his main theme—the importance of love for the human psyche. The development began as far back as the baby in the womb. The mother's mental peace was very important during this time. And later, he said, the child's body and brain are both developed by affectionate touch. All this showed that "humanity really needed affection." And then he linked the development of human love to our attitude to the planet, by calling on another simple metaphor. "Sometimes I call our planet our mother. Our mother planet is telling us, 'My dear children, behave in a more harmonious way. Please take more care of me.' " Behaving more harmoniously with each other and taking more care of the Earth were immediately linked.

We had to give more serious consideration to long-term interests—and to take personal responsibility. "The time has come to think very carefully in these matters. We can't blame a few troublemakers—politicians, or fanatics. It is the business of every human being to have responsibility—a sense of universal responsibility." He pointed to the important role the media could play, giving proper guidance. We also needed a "proper educational system for the younger generation." A child's mind needed to sense the importance of human qualities and human values as a reality.

He was emphatic on this point: the importance of developing a clear realization in a child's mind of the values of love and compassion. It seemed to me that that was what he had done for us, too, during his talk. He had not merely offered words—difficult, abstract concepts that our minds struggled to understand; rather, he had spoken very simply, using his manner, his voice, his whole deportment, to present as a real experience the truth of what he wanted us to grasp. His face, his behavior, all expressed the lively warmth and affection that he spoke of. He was talking of a way of being, and he seemed to be it.

Love, as His Holiness had described it, was essential for our inner well-being—and essential for our outer well-being, since our loving attitude affects everyone and everything we come into contact with, including, eventually, the planet itself. At present, it seemed, we had created a feedback loop of aggression and mistrust; we needed to replace it with a loop of affection.

It was time to end his speech. The Dalai Lama had talked of religion as something that gives us a contribution to offer, something to practice ourselves, not a dogma to impose on anyone else. He practised what he preached in the way he closed: "If you agree with some of these thoughts," he said, "try to implement them yourself. Otherwise—just forget it!" And, as we all broke into laughter, he bowed respectfully to the audience and sat down, smiling.

There was a short question time after the Dalai Lama's speech but the range of questions he was allowed to answer was strictly circumscribed by the British government, which had granted him entry into the country only on condition that he kept away from political discussions. He was not allowed to discuss the Sino-Tibetan situation; he was here strictly as a spiritual leader of Buddhists, not as a political leader of Tibetans. It was a grim reminder of realpolitik's harshness: at the conference we might be learning to say yes to each other, to connect in an attitude of love and respect that overcame barriers, but outside this special receptacle the dominant word was still no.

The first questioner avoided concrete politics: in fact, she went to the opposite extreme, and didn't ask a question at all. In a voice filled with adoration, she requested to hear His Holiness speak in his native language. I blushed with embarrassment, but His Holiness, too compassionate to indulge in the criticism that embarrassment implied, complied.

The next questioner caused a ruckus. A sturdily built man in a smart business suit strode into the center of the aisle and began to shout. The atmosphere of cosy warmth in the hall immediately evaporated. "The microphones aren't working!" he cried out. "They've been switched off!" He was convinced there was a conspiracy to prevent him from addressing the conference. He began to call out a string of political slogans, beginning with the low pay of nurses in Oxford and ending with "Troops out of Northern Ireland!" as security men steered him out of hearing. The press leapt to their feet, cameras flashed furiously, and the man dispensed sheafs of papers wrapped in a blue cover before he was removed.

I ran up to him for a sheaf, which turned out to be a home-made booklet of poems. The man was Patrick Duffy, a trade union official, and the poems were his own. They expressed the confusion and powerlessness all of us at the conference had felt, faced with global disasters:

> My brain is crowded with pain,
> I am separated with surgical precision from meaning,
> I am simply left waiting.

Some participants were angry that the man should have
barged in so aggressively. Others were bothered: were we being
too cosy in here, while in the "real" world people like this banged
their heads on brick walls? Others just shrugged. "You always get
demonstrators like this at conferences." The intruder had put his
message over in such an aggressive way that he was almost bound
to be rejected (possibly confirming for him a prejudice that he
would be rejected because we were too smug to care). Perhaps, I
thought, his passion needed to be tempered with more discrimi-
nation—but then again, too many of us seemed so damned dis-
criminating that our passion congealed in our veins. At least he
cared enough to risk making a spectacle of himself.

The opposite of love, his action shamed me into remembering,
was not hate but indifference. Anyone who was engaged in the
process of making the world fairer, even if they set about it in a
hopeless way, was more a friend than a person who was too
"sophisticated" to try. Change was vital, in the true sense of the
word. Stasis was death.

Later that day, in a television interview, the Dalai Lama spoke
feelingly about the less powerful members of society: "Always,
[the] weaker section [is the] number one casualty. Sad, very sad.
The voice of the weaker section cannot reach the other area unless
someone makes violence—very sad, you see.

"Killing, bleeding . . . I feel violence, torture—these are
inhuman. But nobody pays attention unless some very sad things
happen." He indicated that the leaders who don't pay attention to
people unless they resort to violence have a measure of responsibility for that violence.

I wondered what would have happened if, instead of security
guards hustling away the man, the Dalai Lama had been allowed
to deal with him personally. Would letting the man stay have
resulted in nothing more than a discourtesy to His Holiness—or
might some small human miracle have happened?

Later, I heard that some of the delegates had been to visit the
poet. So perhaps he felt his voice had been heard after all. I hoped
so.

This need of the "voice of the weaker section to reach the
other area," as the Dalai Lama had put it, also exercised another

political leader: Manuel Ulloa, former prime minister of Peru. I listened to his speech from the platform on Wednesday, spoke to him briefly at the conference, and again at some length many weeks later.

His theme was constant: like the Dalai Lama, he was concerned about the responsibility of leaders to the ordinary citizen— in the original sense of the leaders' "response-ability." How "able-to-respond" did he think our present political leaders were to the people they governed? Not nearly responsive enough, was his view: the present political systems are too slow and egoistic. And, as the people become more aware of their rights, they are beginning to show their discontent.

"There is an acute problem of leadership," he said. "There is a disconnection between the political system and the realities that we face. We talk on different wavelengths. And this creates a vacuum that is always filled with something or somebody—maybe with violence, or with the loss of hope. People have more and more the need to be governed in a more simple, direct, humble way."

The same narrowing of the gap was necessary, in his view, between the people and their spiritual leaders. "People need to receive the spiritual message in a less dogmatic way. There needs to be greater humility and a desire to open a multisectoral dialogue. Throughout the world there is a greater consciousness of the need to have a different type of debate."

The emphasis, then, was on talking and listening in a new way—a way that allowed alternative points of view to be genuinely heard; it was very different from the old manner of governing, where the leaders imposed their policies on the people and the people obeyed. What had brought about this consciousness of the need for dialogue instead of dogma? Was it "the terror" that Tom Berry had spoken of?

"Well, for sure, one thing is the brink of disaster," said Ulloa. "But also the pressure from poor people. With the opening of communications, with the better understanding of the world, there is a perception by the people that they have a voice, that they have a right. With satellite television, more education, you see what happens in Algeria, in China, in this country, everywhere. Things are moving because people *know*, because they associate themselves with a worldwide process of balanced justice, protection of animal life, vegetable life, natural resources."

So were we talking about the empowerment, the raised consciousness, of ordinary citizens, who were beginning to see that they have a right to have a say in the management of the world, to have a role in the world?

"Yes. They are beginning to take a presence. In Mexico, for example, there has been for many years a very peculiar political system, very rigid, very selfish, only concerned with political privileges for some and the economics that went with supporting those privileges. All of a sudden younger people, new people, have shown their presence—they have become conscious of what their real rights are, their real expectations, because of their inner meditation and introspection. And without major violence we have had a real revolution after almost fifty years."

What did he mean by "a real revolution"? Mexico's old ruling party was still in office, although nudged out of complacency by the close finish at the last election. Ulloa meant an inner revolution, a revolution of attitude in the manner of leadership, "not imposing one dogma, whether military or political or economic, which by definition must suppress someone else in order to keep that power."

He offered as another example the situation in Chile, where the cast-iron manacle of General Pinochet's dictatorial regime has been loosened after a decade and a half. "Today the Chileans, in a very responsible way, with understanding and humility, have been holding a dialogue between the people who have won and the people who are afraid of another violent change."

He made clear that by political change he wasn't talking about replacing one angry ape, so to speak, with another, but about a new consciousness that sprang from a spiritual dimension, the glassy essence. At this level there was the possibility of barriers falling, gaps narrowing. When I asked him, some weeks after the conference, what had been the effect on him of being at Oxford, he thought for a moment and said, "I feel more with the people." I pressed him further: did he mean that instead of governing the people through control, he had a feeling of being one with them? He nodded and spoke of "more compassion."

"Com-passion"—didn't that mean "suffering with"? That was

quite a change for a leader, to move from a vertical relationship with his constituency to a horizontal one: from the traditional position of high patriarchal control to suffering among the people; to use a spiritual metaphor, to move from firepower to the power of tears. How far he had moved in this direction I couldn't say, but for a politician even to see it as a desirable direction seemed to me good news. It was a far cry from the attitude of most of the leaders in the country of my birth, or indeed the present leaders of my adopted country.

Ulloa talked passionately in his speech at Oxford about violence and inequality. He spoke of such obvious forms of violence in the world as terrorism or war—but also of institutionalized violence. He cited the bitterness felt by the poor nations of the South because of the injustice of international trade patterns imposed by the North. And he emphatically denounced the lie that is used to justify another kind of structural violence: "the pretense of racial superiority."

During the holocaust of World War Two, he said, by means of this rationalization "the so-called civilized world, especially the 'most civilized' world, committed acts of barbarism and savagery that caused millions of deaths and sorrow, pain, and destruction in a way unparalleled in the history of humanity. . . . I believe man has to give up his own internal divisions and do away with the feeling that racial, national, religious, cultural, or economic superiority can be a basis on which humanity can live in peace."

"Man has to give up his own internal divisions"—the phrase made me sit up. Did we have here a politician who didn't blame the enemy outside for everything, but was prepared to look inside himself for the source of the shadow falling on the planet? And prepared to advise his constituency to look inside themselves too? I asked him later about these internal divisions. Did he agree that people tended to avoid the violence inside themselves and to project it entirely onto others, instead of recognizing and taking responsibility also for their own inner violence? He replied with an example.

> We have a very violent movement in Peru called "Shining Path." For many years we believed that it was basically a movement associated with fanaticism. [In

other words, the violence had been perceived in the
past as located only in a fanatic's psyche. It didn't
implicate those of us belonging to a "sane" society.] But
gradually, as we have been forced to look into [the issue
of violence]—because violence has touched all of us, it
has come into the whole community—people have mobilized themselves and tried to understand what was
happening. We are beginning to see that fanaticism
cannot provoke the kind of following that Shining Path
has. . . . This is a responsibility and challenge for
everybody, to look at ourselves and say, "Something is
wrong here. What is it that we have done to create this?
What can we do to avoid the civil war?"

Instead of pushing the shadow of violence completely outside the
socially acceptable group and onto "them," it seems that Peruvian
society is beginning to look into itself to see its part in the creation
of that violence. It reminded me of the words of the Dalai Lama:
"We can't blame a few troublemakers—politicians, or fanatics. It is
the business of every human being to have responsibility—a sense
of universal responsibility."

This theme of taking personal responsibility for the common
good ran throughout the conference. Princess Elizabeth of Yugosla-
via, another delegate, offered a variation of an old slogan: "Think
globally, act locally—and commit individually." But if every individual on the planet is expected to feel a personal responsibility
for the universal good, they must also be able to count on the right
to be respected as being fully human themselves.

Responsibilities and rights are two sides of the same coin.
Charlotte Waterlow said: "The Universal Declaration of Human
Rights may be regarded as the moral code of the modern age.
Almost every society everywhere is struggling to implement these
rights." And Señor Perez de Cuellar, secretary general of the
United Nations, had said in a message to the conference: "How do
we . . . seek to assure the future for the generations that follow? I
am firmly of the conviction that we have to apply the principles
. . . which are embodied in the Universal Declaration of Human
Rights."

What are these human rights? And what is significant about

their rise to prominence now? Those of us who live politically sheltered lives in the West often associate the phrase "human rights" with the drama of prisoners of conscience; we think of Nelson Mandela, or Soviet dissidents sent to Siberia. We are lucky enough to be able to take for granted "everyday" human rights that others cannot.

"The specific rights proclaimed in the Universal Declaration are well known," Charlotte Waterlow had written in a paper she gave me.

> Freedom of speech, assembly, travel, worship, to form associations, to have a fair trial and so on; the political right to take part in the government of one's country; and the social rights to a decent standard of living and to education.
>
> Included in the list is the right of men and women freely to choose their marriage partners, and to enjoy equal rights during marriage and at its dissolution. (Article 16.) In the Western world we tend to take these rights for granted as a norm for social development. We do not realise that their philosophical basis is revolutionary: the simple concept that they belong to persons, as such, because the purpose of human life is "the full development of the human personality" (article 26[2]). . . .
>
> Traditional societies, with the partial exceptions of those of ancient Greece and Rome, were organised on the basis of the idea that the purpose of an individual's life wasn't to develop his or her personal creativity, but to perform his or her duties as a cell in the social organism—as a peasant, a scholar, a warrior, a landowner, a priest, a housewife or a courtesan. In traditional Japan, a person who behaved in an "other-than-to-be-expected way" could be executed. In traditional East Africa an expression of personal originality led to ostracism from the tribe, a fate worse than death.
>
> In traditional India a similar fate befell anyone who broke the innumerable rules of the 3,000 sub-castes; at the end of her life, Gandhi's sister cursed her great

brother for condeming her "to a life-time of humiliation
and ostracism by the people about whom she minded,
the orthodox of her own subcaste and neighbourhood",
because he broke all the caste rules and attacked the
whole system. The concept of human rights is explosive. . . .

Perhaps, therefore, the key question for the modern
world is: who is a person?

If the answer is "everyone"—if humanity were genuinely to accept
every human being as entitled to full human rights, then the main
rationalizations propping up racism, sexism, colonialism, and dis-
crimination against people with disability, as well as a great deal
of child abuse, would melt away.

But where is such an answer to come from? It would take too
long to wait for it to trickle down from political leaders. Several
participants saw more hope in change emerging from the people
themselves. Soedjatmoko, the former rector of the UN University,
saw the devolution of centralized national power as "part of a
general process of increasing global awareness . . . [the initiative
for which comes] from grassroots movements, whose lead governments then will have to follow. The labor movement, the liberation
movements, the women's movement, the environmental movement, the peace movement, are examples of this process."

People's movements: that was a major energy for change in
the world today. Tarzie Vittachi, a journalist due to speak at the
conference on Thursday morning, wrote in a preconference article:

> While scientists look desperately for medicines and me-
> chanisms to avoid catastrophe, many others are begin-
> ning to realise that what is needed is not only externally
> administered remedies, preventive or curative, but an
> internal change in the way we behave, a hard second
> look at the values which have brought us to this danger-
> ous brink.
>
> This concern is being discussed in millions of
> homes, in social groups and even within political parties
> where the prevailing notions such as what is moral is
> what "works" and what is good is what is profitable,
> that power over others obtained by the possession of

increasingly deadlier weapons justifies their production and deployment, that it is reasonable to spend $1½ trillion of the world's treasure on those weapons when nearly a billion people, half of them children, are destitute, are being challenged.

A groundswell of public confidence is rising. Ordinary people are no longer content to believe that we should tamely be manoeuvered by people in power. We need our leaders to play a different role: to stand as barriers for us against powerful negative interests while we rethink and rechoose the values by which the world is run; we know we have something to offer. We are not liabilities but assets, given the chance to think and be heard.

The recently raised interest in the environment is a prime example of the people pressing forward and the leaders being obliged to follow. As Manuel Ulloa put it, people are asking questions, and politicians are embarrassed by not knowing the answers, so they have to find out.

In Brazil, for example, public pressure and commercial interests are locked hand-to-hand over the cutting down of the rain forests—and Brazil's president has had to announce that he will take steps to protect the trees. In the U.S., according to Tom Berry, there are now some twelve thousand environmental groups, with hundreds more being added every year; the presidential candidates are having to include mentions of ecology in their debates, even though they don't recognize the central importance of what is happening. In Britain, after years of lobbying by public-interest groups, the government has—in the autumn after the Oxford conference—at last discovered the greenhouse effect and the ozone layer; suddenly ecology is headline news, though the information is often used for short-term political ends rather than to engender a genuine, far-reaching commitment to global survival. But it's a start.

A Christian Aid leaflet available at the conference summed up the new role conscientious leaders could play, not as controllers of mindless masses, but as supporters of the strength and wisdom and talent that ordinary people can offer when they are given a chance:

> The majority of the world's people have scarcely enough
> to keep them alive. They have little or no say in what

happens to them. Unlike the strong they cannot protect or further their own interests.

We cannot be content to alleviate their suffering. It must be brought to an end. The world, we believe, is likely to be a fairer place where strength is not left to take advantage of weakness but is balanced by strength.

We must act strategically to strengthen the arm of the poor until they can stand up to those who so often act against them, and have the power to determine their own development under God.

We can forget the destitute have many gifts. So often "rich in things and poor in soul," we have much to receive from their hands.

Charity, then, is not a matter of the rich patronizingly throwing down a little loose change at the poor. Charity is restored to its proper meaning of "love": it is a horizontal, nor a vertical, exchange. In the union that comes with love, we see poor people as ourselves; and we recognize their full potential as gifts that could be offered to the world if they were not crushed out of existence.

Part of the planetary therapy seemed to involve a reframing of the political relationship between the powerful and the powerless, that is, between political leaders and their constituencies, or more affluent members of the planet and the poorer ones. And that reframing involves a movement away from dominance, control, a sense of superiority and separation leading to selective deafness, toward equality, connection, openness, and listening.

Dr. Ariyaratne, the dynamic and irrepressible founder of Sarvodaya Shramadana, the Sri Lankan people's development movement, has in his workshop a notice that says cheerfully: "Every mouth to be fed is linked to a pair of hands and a talented brain." If we heal our pathological culture, we may at last cease to see other people only as angry apes threatening the planet and start to welcome them as bearers of essential talents.

8 *Spiritual Listening*

> There is no stopping place in this life. No, nor was
> there ever one, for anyone no matter how far along
> the way they've come. This, then, above all things:
> Be ready for the gifts of God, and always for new
> ones.
>
> MEISTER ECKHART

Dr. Robert Runcie, the Archbishop of Canterbury, is a great
believer in the therapeutic value of talking and listening. Every
year, for many years, he has spent a few days ensconced in
spiritual retreat with the same close friends. In this environment
they pause to look at the present state of their inner journey:
where are they now in their understanding? What do they really
believe?

These occasions the Archbishop finds intensely rewarding. It
would be impossible for him to search his soul under the public
gaze, where the greedy eye of the news camera hunts for cracks in
the archepiscopal armor. So he turns instead to a group that
functions in very much the same way as a therapy group. A trusted
circle of people, all focusing their attention on one subject of
interest and concern to them, can create an atmosphere in which
they can divest themselves of their simplified public certainties
and enter, together, the arena of uncertainty.

In an interview at the conference, the Archbishop made plain
the importance he placed on this kind of dialogue: "There are
complications in our world today, so anybody who tries to over-
simplify is in real danger. [We need] greater understanding and
respect for truth among us. Truth has been rather a casualty in a
lot of world debate. If there is reverence for truth and reverence for
each other, and we are turned in the same direction, you may be
surprised at what happens."

One key element, then, is reverence for each other. If we are not held in a mutually respectful and loving relationship, the transformation will not take place: we will be too busy defending ourselves to hear each other. Reverence for the truth is another element, for again it means that we will be too attached to our own truth—in other words, to our old truth—to be prepared to reach for new insights. And third, we must be turned in the same direction: that is to say, the context the group holds in common needs to be clearly and mutually understood even though the individual contributions each person brings may be very different.

In these respects, could the Oxford conference be seen as a good therapy group? We were certainly turned in the same direction, for our context, global survival, was vividly held. As for reverence for truth and reverence for each other, many of us had already come to feel a high degree of trust and respect for people we had met at Oxford. The hothouse atmosphere at international conferences always compresses the time it takes to make intense relationships. But other things contributed too, like the friendliness of delegates whom one might have expected to find inaccessible or intimidating. For instance, when I asked James Lovelock rather nervously whether he could spare a few minutes to be interviewed, he came and sat on the floor of my study, warming his frozen feet by the fire—even fine April days in England are chilly—and we fell into conversation like old friends for the best part of the afternoon.

The informality of living in spare student quarters at an undergraduate college, rather than at a smooth and shiny conference center, also broke down barriers—six political and spiritual leaders sharing one bleak bathroom ("Can you pass me the towel, Rabbi?") isn't conducive to condescension. And instead of the bland professionalism of conference staff, we had the freshness of student volunteers to help us find our way around.

This was all deliberate policy. The conference organizers emphatically didn't want the conference "to be like UN conferences." They were familiar with organizing those, but this time they wanted a conference where people didn't hide behind their national or religious banners, feeling like representatives or lobbyists for those fixed points of view. They wanted to make it as easy as possible for people to move forward with all the vulnerability and complexity of the human individuals they were.

86

Another crucial element, if people are going to speak freely, is confidentiality. Although the morning speeches in Oxford Town Hall were recorded on film and tape by the international media, the afternoon sessions were quite different: we met in five smaller groups in scattered rooms to share our thoughts with no media present. We could talk and listen without anyone feeling obliged to play to the camera. The politicians, especially, seemed relieved by this freedom.

But having talked and listened, then what? Would we try to put together the ingredients we had heard from everyone to make one giant pudding of an answer to the problems of global survival? Or would one slender answer, a golden core of agreement, rise shiningly through, while the rest fell away? Or would there be some third possibility?

The Archbishop of Canterbury was firm: "If we suppose that we can all agree—then we shall have, out of a conference like this, a shapeless blancmange." He didn't believe in the emergence of one whole and final answer, whether plump or thin. "There are those who feel that the world is in desperate need of a new and larger vision of unity which transcends existing differences.

"There are dangers here, as well as hope. In a recent lecture on the pursuit of the ideal, Sir Isaiah Berlin drew a distinction between the quest for a perfected and unified world—a good and noble pursuit—and the temptation to translate this vision into reality by taking short cuts. Sir Isaiah chillingly recalls that this temptation forms the genesis of each and every final solution."

The import of the phrase "final solution" was not lost on the conference participants. Dr. Runcie continued: "So we are warned not to think that resistance to our goal is always mistaken. There are genuine differences in the apprehension of truth. Ignorance and malevolence are not to be imputed as the characteristics of those who disagree with us." He had dashed from our lips the cup that contained the hope of a simple, universal solution. What did he offer instead? We had to keep talking, he said, "as partners in a continuing dialogue about the meaning and purpose of life."

So what was so special about dialogue? How could a continuing dialogue help global survival? Wasn't it what we arrived at through talking, rather than how we arrived at it, that mattered— the outcome, rather than the process? At the start of the conference, most of the delegates I spoke to assumed, like me, that a strong concrete solution to global problems was what we were aiming to find by the end of the conference week. But here was the Archbishop laying stress on the process and being very mysterious about the outcome: "If we get together in a spirit of listening and cooperating, despite our different secular and spiritual experiences, and if we don't behave like know-alls but as people who are ready to receive all, then we may make some progress."

Even more mysteriously, the conference organizers, despite their years of hard work, weren't asking for a concrete outcome. They presented no agenda for the conference and sought no product at the end of it. Other conferences usually went further down the opposite line; not only did they require an outcome, they often had it decided and written up before the conference began. The process of these conferences was merely one of rubber-stamping a preformulated solution. No spontaneous changes were expected or even welcomed. A few delegates might have to be coaxed to move from point A to the desired point B, but everyone else knew very well where point B was, and what it consisted of, and had long since moved there.

This conference was different because we genuinely didn't know what point B was—and one of the purposes of the conferences was, it seemed to me, to acknowledge that we didn't. Political and spiritual leaders were people who traditionally had the right answers—that's what we consulted them for. And yet, we now had to admit, the old answers they had offered hadn't led us to peace and harmony. They had led us to war.

Perhaps the first purpose of the conference, then, was to acknowledge universally that no one—not any single one of the political or religious systems represented here—already held the right answer. That in itself was a revolutionary admission. It immediately took away from any of the leaders here the right to dominate the others with their way of seeing; it melted away the age-old self-righteousness used to justify holy wars.

What this conference offered was not a platform for leaders of different sectarian groups to argue for each of their solutions being the best, but a place where they could frankly admit that none of their solutions had proved adequate by themselves. They had all failed, in effect, to solve the problems of global survival. Something new had to be found. One participant, a journalist, said: "It felt like walking onto an empty tennis court. You can hear the echoes of past players—but the court has been cleared, ready for a new game."

The organizers were trying to create a framework within which people could speak openly, saying whatever they felt it was important to say. Whatever arose from that dialogue was the best that could arise at this moment and from this group of people, and they were prepared to accept it. Their business was to invite the most committed, enthusiastic, knowledgeable leaders they could find from the political and spiritual realms, put them together in a sympathetic space for a week, and see what happened spontaneously.

If the participants wanted some plan or resolution to emerge at the end of the conference, something concrete, that was up to them; the organizers weren't pressing for it. In the event, there was a brief declaration. Some people loved it; others found it a little woolly and suggested ways to strengthen it. During its drafting, Akio Matsumura, the executive coordinator whose idea the conference had originally been, declined invitations to be on the drafting committee. And when he made his formal welcoming speech at the start of the conference, it lasted less than five minutes. In the speech he asked us for detachment from our habitual stances so that we could listen well. For the rest of the conference, he sat quietly and listened well. Other members of the organization kept an even lower profile—they worked tirelessly all through the conference but off-stage and out of sight.

This detachment was baffling to many outside the organization. Before we put on a play we like to ensure we'll be applauded for it. To summon an audience and title the play, only to allow the actors, who have never met before, to improvise spontaneously seems a highly risky business. Many of his Western friends were so puzzled, Akio Matsumura said, that they tried to persuade him to formulate some idea at least of the outcome the organizing committee wanted. He appreciated their kindness—they were trying to be protective in the manner of their own culture (which, he insisted, was not wrong of them)—but to be goal oriented would be to miss the point of the kind of conference the organizers wanted. He insisted that there must be no pressure to have a concrete outcome of any kind. The organizers must only offer a sympathetic space in which something—or nothing—might happen.

The best way I could understand this extraordinary detachment was to remember the experience of a friend I'd recently made, an elderly woman named Rachel Pinney. She used to go on "Ban the Bomb" marches in the 1960s, but she soon realized that the more she tried to convince onlookers of her antibomb views, the more their position became polarized and fixed in opposition. One night she had a powerful dream in which she saw all the people of the world living tragically alone in separate underground cells. The dream inspired her to find a method of communication tht could draw people closer together. If talking pushed people apart, she thought, she would stop talking and start listening. She packed up a rucksack, left her medical practice, and started to walk across Britain and the U.S., consciously seeking out people who disagreed with her views. When she found such people, she would make them a promise: that she would listen attentively and respectfully to their views for an agreed length of time, and that she would never argue with them about this subject; not then, not ever. In fact, she would never even raise with them again the subject of their unusual "conversation." Her only response would be to play back at intervals during the dialogue, in her own words, what she thought the speaker had said—just so that if she had misunderstood anything, the speaker would have the chance to correct the misunderstandings.

The results were astonishing. Because her conversational partners were not feeling pressed to defend their views against her views, they were able to lay their views out and then stand back from them. They would re-examine their own views—perhaps for the first time in years; at last they felt free to unhook from and reconsider their old beliefs.

Rachel called this method of change "creative listening" and she has used it ever since as a form of therapy, especially with disturbed children. But it can work for anyone. She tried it on me and it worked with eerie speed. We dealt with a deeply held fear I had; I almost didn't want to speak it out loud to her, but the knowledge that no one, not even Rachel, would ever raise the subject again made it possible to face it for a brief time. But in the moment of stepping back to examine this fear, there was a flicker of freedom and an experience of myself as I was without the weight of the fear pressing on me. I was alive and well, better than before. I didn't need the fear; it was protecting me from nothing worthwhile. It began to lose its hold over me.

It seemed, then, that the Global Forum organizing committee was creating at the Oxford conference a receptacle where we could all have experiences of creative listening, and the release and growth that stems from it. Inner change—metanoia, cultural therapy—could happen at the conference, and through a process of greater freedom, not through the domination of one thinker over another.

It was a highly paradoxical method of transformation, a million miles away from our everyday methods of hard persuasion, which, as often as not, create further conflict: more greed, fear, insecurity, suspicion, aggression, clannish clinging. Hard persuasion homes in on our deepest anxieties—it activates our "angry ape." Creative listening, by contrast, works to free us from the domination of suspicion and aggression, to open us up, bit by bit, to the "glassy essence" in ourselves.

A sentence in the first draft of the conference declaration, presented to the assembled delegates for their approval, read: "Each one of us has been changed by our Oxford experience." The only objection to this line came from a delegate who suggested it should be strengthened to read: "Each one of us has been improved. . . ." A wave of approving laughter came from the assembly.

There was no doubt, from talking to dozens of people at the conference, that many people felt improved. Several found it impossible to explain exactly what the improvement had been—it was a feeling, they said, groping for words, of being revitalized or energized. They felt far more committed than when they had first arrived, even though they had always cared about these issues. No one that I met, even the few who had "20 percent reservations, 80 percent satisfaction" about the conference, regretted the time they had spent at Oxford.

One celebrated delegate who confessed to me that he had kept his bags packed and his excuses ready, prepared to leave immediately after he had given his speech at the start of the week, changed his mind and happily stayed to the end. Another came only as a gesture of support for his wife who was a delegate—and found the conference had a profound effect on his own work in the months that followed. A hardened conference-goer who had decided he was too busy to turn up till the end of the week wished, when he arrived, that he had made the time to come sooner.

The level of enthusiasm was extraordinary: it was not the sort of response I had ever come across before at an international conference. Egotistic displays, competitiveness, cynicism, freeloading, politicking, predatory sexuality, interspersed with a few well-worn phrases that once had idealism alive in them—these were more commonplace sights. Not that Oxford was devoid of any of these tendencies, but for once they didn't dominate.

Looking back on the conference now, two aspects of our "improvement" stand out most strikingly. One was to do with a greater understanding of the human-Earth relationship; the other with a clarification of the distinction between religion and spirituality.

To take the human-Earth relationship first: we had come to see very clearly that the massive environmental and political problems threatening us had been caused by our own misbehavior and, further, that this misbehavior was impelled by a set of attitudes and values that we could encapsulate as belonging to the "angry ape." They included the wish to dominate, to grab territory, to pretend knowledge of what was unknown, to be defensive-aggressive, to be clannish, to preen . . . The common denominator appeared to be egotism. By contrast, we had also been presented with a different set of attitudes and values: a recognition of the importance of humility, equality, inclusion as part of a whole. The common denominator of these qualities appeared to be love.

None of this, so far, was different from the messages that had been given to us by spiritual and ethical leaders for centuries. The new element was this: the Earth was now evoked as the common context for our love. Sagan talked of being a "planetarist"; Lovelock talked of love as the quality that connected his father to the natural world and had the power to reconnect all of us to Gaia; Maathai held a vision of one humanity returning, inexorably as dust, to the Earth.

In evoking a loved Earth as our common context, the scientists welcomed all earthly inhabitants, transcending the old boundary lines of state, class, creed, or species. Significantly, Mother Theresa didn't evoke the Earth to engender love, and she didn't call on love for all its species—she was selective even about which humans she chose to love, at least in theory, though in practice she seemed more universally loving. The dogma seemed to be more selective than the person who lived it. But other spiritual leaders did evoke the Earth, like the Dalai Lama, who heard Mother Earth crying out to her children.

The Archbishop of Canterbury included even more than the Earth—he made it clear that "the whole of creation" was the context he held for love:

> At the present time, when we are beginning to appreciate the wholeness and interrelatedness of all that is in the cosmos, preoccupation with humanity can seem distinctly parochial. We need now to extend the area of the sacred and not to reduce it . . . . The nonhuman parts of creation would then be seen as having an intrinsic value of their own rather than being dependent for value on their relation to human beings.
>
> I believe that all too often our theology of creation, especially here in the so-called developed world, has been distorted by being too man-centered. We need to maintain the value, the preciousness of being human by affirming the preciousness of the nonhuman also—of all that is.
>
> For our concept of God forbids the idea of a cheap creation, of a throwaway universe in which everything is expendable save human existence. The whole universe is a work of love. And nothing which is made in love is cheap. The value, the worth, of natural things is not found in man's view of himself but in the goodness of God who made all things good and precious in his sight.

This is quite a shift. For traditionally, as Father Tom Berry puts it, the great difficulty with the monotheistic religions is that Nature is left out:

Generally the Divine is experienced as an immediate pervasive presence; but when the Bible absorbs that presence and constellates it as a transcendental personal divine being, and then establishes a covenant relationship between humans and the divine, then the natural world is left out. But the natural world is the locus, the normal locus, for the meeting between the human and the divine.

That's why human religious rituals are designed in association with the cosmic ritual. Our celebration days are moments of cosmic change. That's why, particularly in India, it is important to consult the stars, consult the universe, before you do anything. In the Chinese world of the I Ching also, you consult the universe before you do anything.

How could an industrialized world perceive divinity? Scientists, Father Berry said, could teach us to be more sensitive to creation: they could use their instruments to gather information not in the service of mechanistic "progress" but in order to sensitize us to nature, "to help us listen to the voices of the Earth and the rest of creation."

It seemed to me that this open, listening relationship with the Earth offered a two-way change: not only would it help humans to treat the Earth with more care, it could help give humans a sense that we had a legitimate place in the natural system—a less inflated position than the one of conqueror, which we had previously tried to assume, but a more secure one. The more we saw how everything was interconnected, how everyone belonged within a planet-sized ecosystem, the more we knew we had a place in the universe. We belonged to the Earth; if the Earth was our common context, we were no longer homeless adventurer on alien territory.

In traditional societies, anthropologists tell us, strict rituals and customs kept such alienation at bay: at puberty, each child went through a socially honored rite of passage into a ready-made slot in the culture. From early childhood everyone knew what was required of them to be worthwhile members of a coherent society. They were part of a meaningful whole, and the value residing in the whole gave value also to each interconnected part.

Now, however, in an industrial society, value is placed not on the meaning of the whole but on the chutzpah of the individual, striding through the debris of crumbling social structures, every man for himself. The Archbishop of Canterbury put it like this:

> Greed, hedonism, and the lust for power are sometimes the forces which impel technological and scientific progress, culminating in the exploitation of the Earth and its people. Tribal and aboriginal people have often been the victims of such hubris. In my travels over the world, I hear stories about how such people have lost their land and had their social fabric destroyed in the name of progress and development.
>
> Yet it is often the traditional worldview of such people which provides a framework for living in harmonious ways within the created order. There is a sense of the sacredness of the environment in many tribal and aboriginal communities. Such societies offer an understanding of the world which is based on the interrelatedness of the human and the nonhuman, the animate and the inanimate.

But there is no way back to a preindustrial society for most of us, even if that is what we should want. Yet we do want a social context that gives us a larger meaning. Was being a "planetarist" where we would find it?

From most of the speakers so far we had received a similar message: they perceived the Earth as a whole, as our common context. They felt themselves to be members of their tribal group and, simultaneously, a member of the planet. They modeled a new planetary consciousness. This seemed to be, at the Oxford conference, the way forward.

The second point that had been clarified for me at the conference was the distinction between religion and spirituality. Dr. Ariyaratne explained it like this:

> When we speak of religion, it is very important that we make a clear distinction between religion in its outer form and in its inner content. Most people attach them-

selves to the outer form of religion, with its traditions, customs, and practices. We may even call this outer form the material culture of religion. On the other hand, the inner content of religion consists of qualities such as respect for life, compassion, contentment, forgiveness, and peace. This inner content of religion may be called the spiritual culture of religion.

When followers of religion give more importance to their external form or the material culture, conflicts are bound to arise. Therefore the inner content loses its vitality and religion becomes another factor that divides human beings into conflicting groups. History abounds with instances of such conflicts, which have led to violence, misery, and destruction of human lives. . . .

Religion devoid of its spiritual content is sometimes worse than any other materialistic ideology that divides human beings, leading to violence and destruction. It is not possible to bring about any worthwhile and sustainable unity and cooperation among religions unless the spiritual content of religions is given more importance. In other words, the most critical challenge of our times is the awakening of spirituality. . . .

Concepts like unity, cooperation, and compassion become concrete realities only when man transcends the outer form and delves deep into the inner spirit of a human personality. Only spiritual awakening in human beings irrespective of their religious motivation can bring about lasting cooperation.

As I am a Buddhist, like one in any other religion, I have to follow certain customs, practices, and traditions. These may be performed in a mechanical way, providing me with psychological security as an individual belonging to a larger group. At this mechanical level there is hardly anything I have in common with followers of other religions who have other forms of worship, traditions, customs, and practices. . . .

In the outer manifestation of religion there will always be differences that are difficult to reconcile. So at this level I do not think true cooperation is possible. A kind of temporary coexistence, or a state of no war, while the parties are fully armed, is possible. But this is not true peace. For true peace to be there, readiness with arms has to be replaced with a deeper spiritual arsenal of understanding.

I am sure that all religions in their essence have teachings that go deep into human consciousness. At these levels, external forms become increasingly less important. . . . Therefore, instead of religious cooperation, a kind of spiritual communion can come into being in the affairs of people.

When we were looking at religious values at the conference, we were being asked to transcend the particular content of our religious traditions—or rather, to transcend our attachment to them, so that we can go through them and beyond to a universal spiritual level. Dr. Ariyaratne's words echoed those of Dr. Runcie in his Younghusband Memorial Lecture of 1986:

I am not advocating a single-minded, synthetic model of world religions. What I want is for each tradition, especially my own, "to break through its own particularity," as Paul Tillich put it. The way to achieve this "is not to relinquish one religious tradition for the sake of a universal concept which would be nothing but a concept. The way is to penetrate into the depths of one's own religion, in devotion, thought and action. In the depth of every living religion there is a point at which the religion itself loses its importance, and that to which it points breaks through its particularity, elevating it to spiritual freedom and to a vision of the spiritual presence in other expressions of the ultimate meaning of man's existence. That is what Christianity must encounter with the world's religions."

This kind of ecumenism, or "spiritual planetarism," does not require individuals to abandon the outer material forms of their personal religions, only to transcend their attachments to these material forms, working through them to a dimension of spiritual unity. It parallels political planetarism, which requires people to remain members of a particular tribe but go beyond that attachment so that they can become citizens of the whole planet as well.

Jack Blessington, a CBS television producer filming the conference, was stirred by these ideas. Being at the conference had made him think, he said, of the world his children, and his children's children, might inherit. And he made a very perceptive comment: It was difficult sometimes to think in very large, abstract terms of the whole world and of the distant future. But if we thought of our immediate circle, faces of people we know, our children and our grandchildren, then it is possible to think through our love for them to the future they might have to endure. Through the particular, the well known, we can make a link to the distant unknown. As Edmund Burke said two centuries ago, "To be attached to the subdivision, to love the little platoon we belong to in society, is the first principle (the germ, as it were) of affection."

We didn't need to suppress shame-facedly our attachment to our small, intimate circle, our homebase; only to remember to look through it like a telescope lens to understand the larger circle. I thought of the North American Indians' attachment to the patches of land on which they build their homes; through this attachment they understand the importance of land everywhere. And through our individual religious experiences, we can recognize the spirituality in others.

At the conference, then, we had stopped eulogizing the idea of a single perfection, a one right way, which leads to competitive voices shouting each other down till just one voice wins. We had moved towards an ideal of wholeness and cooperation, where everyone listens to each other. The kind of cooperation being suggested here, however, was not the same as consensus arrived at by compromise. For in this sort of consensus, only one voice still prevails; and the owners of the other voices let go their real wishes and agree to compromise.

At Oxford we were trying to go beyond a one-voice consensus to a communion where different voices could be welcome simultaneously, held in a harmony like the different notes of a chord, or the rays emanating from the sun, like the many religions held by one spirituality, the different species inhabiting one Earth, the different cells making up one body. A liver cell is different from a heart cell, and always is; it never compromises itself to become a consensual "body cell." Each cell develops as uniquely itself, and yet each in its difference "knows" the whole body and its place in it. When it is deaf to such knowing it starts to colonize cancerously, and both cell and body die. If we are to survive on the globe, it is this acceptance of differences, coexisting within an awareness of the whole, that we must find.

Dr. Runcie welcomed difference. He said, "A lot of interreligious debate tends to be about removing obstacles. I look upon a gathering like this as an opportunity for the sharing of gifts."

I must admit to being surprised by one form of "welcoming difference" at the conference: people seemed to derive so much pleasure from the different costumes in evidence—maroon-and-ocher Tibetan robes, black Orthodox cassocks and white Dominican habits, pale silk saris, bright cotton African robes, Texan jeans and cowboy hats, power-dressing suits with pearl tie-pins, and others I've never seen before, like the brilliant orange and gold costume, complete with pentagonal hat, worn by the priest from Ulan Bator.

I would have expected such a sophisticated, well-travelled group to be more blasé. But I suppose our multicolored look did offer a vivid image of what our presence at the conference meant. We had been invited to the conference because we represented (even through our clothes) very different cultures, as well as a common concern for the survival of the planet; we expressed diversity and unity together.

One afternoon I asked James Lovelock how he thought we could find out, in a postindustrial age, the way we ought to live. How could each of us discover what we should do, as our individual contribution towards the well-being of the planet? Lovelock refused point-blank to offer a universal prescription; he could only follow the path that he felt was appropriate for him. He lived in a way that made him fulfilled and contented—in the country, planting trees. He couldn't speak for anyone else.

But was it all right, I persisted, to follow a path just because it makes us feel fulfilled and contented inside—wasn't that giving in to selfishness? Didn't an awareness of Gaia mean that we should deny our individual needs, sacrifice them to the general good? The answer came in the form of another question: how, except through

99

an indefinable inner sense of rightness, could an individual know what in their life they could offer for the good of the whole?

We struggled for a metaphor that resolved this apparent conflict and we arrived at this: a body cannot be healthy if its individual cells are wretched. Each cell needs to be happy and healthy for the whole to be so. There is no essential conflict between the needs of a sensitive cell and the needs of the whole body; their interests are the same.

The key, I suppose, lay in the idea of a sensitive cell, one that listened to the whole, as distinct from the cancerous cell that grew, heedless of its neighbors. What was there in us that could help us to hear? One of the participants, Dr. Jyoti, professor emeritus at Punjab University, shared with me the Hindu metaphor for the process of inner growth that allows us to be in contact with the whole. He spoke of the chakras, inner energy centers we all have in a line from the bottom of the spine up to the crown of the head. One of these centers is the solar plexus, and this is where our self-protective, egotistic fears reside, our personal longings and need for belonging, our insecurity and craving for a safe home and for being loved. This is the home of personal feelings, which are not "bad"; they are a part of being human, which includes being vulnerable and needy for love and security.

Further up the line is the heart center. This center is also concerned with love, but it is not about egocentric love. This is the place of love for humanity. It is open, generous, inclusive. It feels the pain of the world, and longs to assuage it. From the heart center flows the energy that impels fellowship, solidarity, communion.

It seems to me that the chakra model pictured with beautiful simplicity the shift of values that the conference was reaching for: the shift from operating at the ego-bound level of the solar plexus, the level at which we could behave like angry apes, to operating altruistically from the heart: a heart that could empathize with and include, but also go beyond, the egotism of the solar plexus.

But what enabled someone to move from one level to another? We couldn't have a million inspiring Oxford conferences. How were those of us who didn't yet feel this "heart" level of planetary consciousness to learn how to respond from there? Even if we accepted the idea intellectually, there would be resistance in our feelings. We were accustomed to operating partially, in small tribal groups or as isolated individuals, not acting as members of an integrated planet. Individuals found themselves torn even within themselves, one inner voice fighting for supremacy over another. There was little sense of trustworthy wholeness in our everyday experience.

In times of danger we shrank even farther into our familiar hiding places. We became more introverted—more tribal, not less. Under threat, we barricaded the door, and pushed a rifle out of the kitchen window to scare off intruders. Gut feelings prevailed, and the gut spoke of personal safety extended only to our nearest and dearest, the people we included as "us" as opposed to "them."

Why should any of this change now—why should we shift from this gut-felt self-protectiveness to a generous, open-hearted vision? No wonder we were confused, like a person wanting to crouch down to protect her soft underbelly while telling herself she ought to stand up and fling her arms wide in welcome. No argument that we ought to feel at one with humanity and the planet at large was going to make us feel that oneness.

Two answers to this question had come from the conference, one negative, one positive. The negative one was the shock of terror, as we saw that we stood teetering on the cliff's edge of global disaster. This must force us out of our small-mindedness. And the positive answer was inner healing. As we felt empowered by being listened to with reverence, we might also empower ourselves by listening to ourselves in the same way, shaking free of our old defenses and props, accepting our small but valued place in the pattern of creation, and offering the Earth the gift of who we truly are.

9 *Justice for Peace*

> I sit on a man's back, choking him and making him carry me, and yet assure myself and others that I am sorry for him and wish to lighten his load by all possible means except by getting off his back.
>
> LEO TOLSTOY

As the ideas I was beginning to understand at the conference became increasingly cosmic and idealistic, I felt anxious to smack them against a little cold reality. I didn't want to leave Oxford on a heroic high, intoxicated by wonderful ideas that shriveled to nothing as soon as they had to be put into practice. So, very late one evening, I invited a handful of participants to meet in my room to share their views on the conference so far—and perhaps to speak more bluntly than they might have in public. One delegate whose views I was particularly eager to hear more fully was Paulos Mar Gregorios, the Metropolitan of Delhi and the North Syrian Orthodox Church of India. His erudition and insight were immense, as I had realized from his cool asides to me between the set speeches. For decades he had been a political leader as well as a spiritual leader: he straddled the realms of both idealism and pragmatism. Since he was not, for once, a platform speaker, and his words were therefore not included in the conference papers, I quote him here at length.

Q: Could this conference lead to anything actually changing?

Metropolitan Gregorios: If we are being asked for practical steps, we could choose a few areas where religion is the ostensible source of conflict—Ireland, for example. In the context of a conference like this, where all the religions of the world are present, we could bring the conflicting parties together so that they could be responsive to a different atmosphere, an atmosphere which is not one of self-justification or accusation or putting the blame on the other, but where we are trying to find together a way out for all of us.

That could be one of the practical things to be done. But it doesn't work in every situation. Where the conflict is between the white regime in South Africa and the black majority, for example, you cannot now go and say "let us sit down and talk to each other"—I think the situation has gone way beyond that stage. In the South African situation the only solution is democracy.

If you have all human beings treated alike, in a democratic situation—that is a solution. It cannot simply be a matter of reconciling two warring parties: where there is clear injustice on the part of one group, then that injustice must be remedied. But in Ireland I think there is more reconciliation needed, because there are faults on both sides, probably, and there are economic factors behind the religious conflict also. In the Middle East, economic factors are very important, the historical factors are very important, but also the religious factor is a source of conflict. There we could use a little more of this kind of atmosphere-creating, which governments cannot do.

I was very much impressed by what Velikhov said about verification problems. They had been talking at a government-to-government level for two years in Geneva—and that ate up a lot of money in hotel bills and champagne bills! But with less than half that money, they organized a conference of scientists on both sides; they knew all the technical details, so they could come to a solution in no time at all.

Something like this may be possible in the Middle East if you have the right kind of atmosphere and the right kind of people participating. You have to have some of the chief authorities of Israel and the Palestinians and the Arab countries all together, but in a different atmosphere than the simply political.

This is just one of the practical, immediate steps for resolving conflict. But that doesn't solve the problem of peace. The roots of war are much deeper.

Most of the European/Western nations are centrally concerned about peace, and now the ecological worry has come, but the justice issue is not at the top of the agenda. For us who come from the Third World the justice issue is primary—and when you talk to us about peace, we say, quite irresponsibly, "That is your

103

problem." It is not; it is not your problem, it is our problem also. But for us the urgency of the justice situation far surpasses the demands of peace and ecology.

It is a different perspective. Well, I am a Christian, and a lot of us have to start from our own religious perspective, then find common ground with other religious views. If we start from our Christian perspective, we find that the doctrine of creation is central to our thinking. If we begin instead with the interpretation of Christianity as a way of saving souls, so to speak, then what happens is a very narrow kind of Christianity.

But if you see God and the whole of creation coming from God—God is not interested only in Christians, God is interested in the whole. And once you get that at the center of the Christian concern, then Christians can be concerned not just about Christians but about all human beings, all animals, everything. So the doctrine of creation is a kind of central framework within which we would look at equality and justice and peace also, because questions of justice and peace are interconnected.

Why is there war? Because some people who are privileged are afraid that their privileges will be taken away—they are the ones who are fighting. The enemies of the establishment are the people who might take away their privileged positions.

The issues of justice and peace are frighteningly interconnected. Peace cannot be discussed the way we have discussed the East/West issue, because quite closely connected with peace is the question of injustice in the world, and the removal of injustice. In the World Council of Churches we have created the slogan, "An unjust peace is just unbearable." We don't want an unjust peace. We don't want everything to be patched up. When there is injustice we don't want to have some kind of a peace which may retain the unjust structures. We want a just peace, not just any peace.

So justice and peace are very closely connected—but neither of them can be separated from the more ecological concern, because if we should ruin our world then we can't have either justice or peace.

Integrally related to each other are: one, a concern for the created order, the whole order; and two, the home as a central interest. And that is the point at which the North American Indian perspective, for example, or the Australian aboriginal perspective, becomes very important in our conference.

Just a couple of months ago, a very articulate Indian said, "You people talk always about time as the most important thing; your God, even, reveals himself to you in time. But for us, it is in space that God reveals Himself; we think of space as the place where we live and where God lives and where everything holds together." Now that is a different perspective. We have to take all these perspectives together and learn from people outside our culture, outside our religion, to think about the whole. Whatever helps us to think about the whole is helpful, and that is why the ecological concern has a kind of priority at the moment.

Q: Because it provides a kind of metaphor by which we can understand the importance of cooperation elsewhere? With ecology it is manifestly clear that only together can we solve the problems. And it forces us to make common cause, whereas if we stayed with the justice and peace issue we could stay forever on different sides within our different traditions.

Metropolitan Gregorios: That is where the report of the UN Commission on Environmental Development, chaired by Mrs. Brundtland, comes in. She was the keynote speaker at a conference we held on justice, peace, and dictatorship. What she was saying is that the present industrial system cannot continue as it is without creating all these problems. So if you want to solve all these problems you must radically revise the system of production and distribution. That's what Mrs. Brundtland says.

Ecological problems are created by the industrial system, injustice is also created by the industrial system, and the people who are benefiting from war are some caucus in the industrial system. It is that system which needs to be thoroughly overhauled.

Q: What can ever persuade us to change?

Metropolitan Gregorios: A change of perspective. Once people begin to see that we can't solve our problems piecemeal, that we are all bound up together in a single world—if that perspective grows, then we should be ready to move from the national to the global in every nation. The tribal people in Africa can move from the tribal to the national; why is it not possible for all the nations in the world to move to the global?

This is the first occasion, the first major occasion, where

parliamentarians and religious leaders have come together on a half-and-half basis to discuss the main problems of the world. And from my perspective, the religious leaders need to speak about spiritual principles—principles that cannot be involved in politics because the rules of the game in politics, as somebody said, will not allow any of these values to be put into that game. That game is played by a separate set of rules. Unless you change the rules of the game in politics you can't put these values into our common life. That is the big bottleneck.

You can talk about values. You can say everyone should be good and everyone should be kind and compassionate and all that—but politics goes on according to a different set of rules. That's where we need to devise a new way of politics, a new way of production and distribution.

This conference as it is now programmed is not likely to produce much substance. What I expect from this conference is a follow-up process, in which substantial, serious strategy is made about the rules of the game of politics; the rules of the game of industrial production; the rules of the game of injustice. Once you have seen those, then you have something on which you can have a discussion locally.

The danger is that if you just bring together a few politicians and a few religious leaders, they will say some nice things, and you will say some nice things, and you will agree—and then you will go home. The perceptions of the religious community are still very naive. They do not understand the complexities of political and economic reality, they are simply talking about values. If you talk like that, the politicians tomorrow will also talk like that, but they will keep on doing what they are doing.

Q: The hard politicians, the realpolitik people are not here. And they are not likely to come.

Metropolitan Gregorios (sadly): Yes . . . Behind the conference are big money organizations. All this is conservative money which has gone into this conference, it is not progressive money and therefore the choice of participants has also been on that scale. There are some people who could speak about the relation between justice and peace in a more informed way and those people have not been brought here. The issue of justice is not central to the thinking of the planners.

Go outside the conference center. Just before you go to the room where you have tea, there are three NATO posters which try to tell you that NATO stands only for peace. NATO doesn't want war, it wants only peace; and the posters say that "if we don't have nuclear weapons Britain will be insecure." Are those posters that somebody has put up for the conference?

Q: Is one of the problems that the mass media are unresponsive to the positive because of their commercial vested interests?

Metropolitan Gregorios: What you are saying is right. I have been in this business for thirty years now. I have dedicated my whole life to it in different jobs. We need to have some understanding of where the great power concentrations are which persist and manipulate our understanding. They make us see reality in a distorted way. They control us.

Newspapers cannot survive unless they get advertisements, and advertisements come from these people. So the newspapers are reluctant; when they say, "This is not news," what they mean is, "We can't afford to publish this because if we do that we lose our advertisements." There was a movement in America that started to find an alternate source of information—from the people themselves—but it has gone, vanished under the weight of the great corporations.

We still have not had the courage to identify who the real villains are at the present time. When you identify them, you will see that most of us are dependent on the structure that promotes injustice.

And so we don't want to go too deeply into the analysis of who really is the beneficiary of the system—because, as the non-starving class of the world from which all of us here are drawn, we are the beneficiaries.

10 *Imprisoned Splendor*

And "to know"
Rather consists in opening out a way
Whence the imprisoned splendor may escape,
Than effecting entry for a light
Supposed to be without.

ROBERT BROWNING

WE had established that all of us at the conference had to learn to transcend our sectarianism and take responsibility for our part in the deepening global disaster. But how was the world at large to be helped to think in this new way? The Dalai Lama, among others, had referred to the important role that schools and journalists could play. Thursday morning's speakers were Soedjatmoko, rector of the UN University, and Tarzie Vittachi, an international journalist. Soedjatmoko believed that education should help new generations to feel secure enough inside themselves to be open to alternative attitudes without feeling threatened:

> We will have to learn that there are multiple ways of perceiving and expressing truth, and to accept the inevitability of religious pluralism and value orientations in this world. . . . [We need] to prepare them for life in a rapidly changing world, in which unpredictability, instability, and vulnerability may well be the commanding features. We will have to develop their capacity to live in such a world without irrational fears or resorting to violence, but with reason and civility . . . without taking refuge in oversimplification, reductionism, dogmatism, or single-issue politics. This may mean a break with the kind of hubris that has characterized much of modern culture. Humankind's racial, cultural, and religious diversity, like the biological diversity on this

planet, ensures rather than reduces the stability of the human race.

Not a single voice, but many; and Soedjatmoko's ideal of many voices included the voices of the dispossessed. "It is obvious that the adjustment of school systems to the global requirements of human survival and solidarity should go way beyond the conventional notions of educational reform."

He spoke of "the need to involve the poor, the marginalized, the illiterate, and the alienated in major learning processes." We had to create a "dense network of interactive social learning environments at all levels of society, capable of involving the rich as well as the poor, the sophisticated as well as the illiterate."

Universities, for instance, are looking at ways to adjust to a changing world, but hardly any are looking at the necessary level: "Very few have begun to organize themselves to deal systematically with the global issues of human survival, development, and welfare . . . and their interrelationship with national problems." And "as under present circumstances nonviolence is no longer a utopian goal, but has become a political necessity," he recommends the teaching in schools of "the historical and contemporary strategy of nonviolence and peace education in general." That's a far cry from the official attitude to peace education in Britain. In a survey written by a Conservative peer, Baroness Cox, and the British New Right's favorite political thinker, Roger Scruton, peace studies were described as "immensely damaging to our national interests and favorable to those of the Soviet Union."

But Soedjatmoko prefers empathy to paranoia. Schools should stimulate the "capacity for empathy and moral imagination. In a period of massive social transformation . . . the human person anywhere in the world is confronted with his need to find meaning in the changes . . . that are affecting his or her life. It forces him to face the fragmentation of his own inner perception of himself and to try to overcome it."

Where does one find guidance for change at this inner level? Soedjatmoko believes "the teaching of ethics would help nurture the sense of inner security, often drawn from faith, that enables one to forgo aggressiveness and violent behavior in situations of great vulnerability."

109

Survival and solidarity have to be on a global, not a national, level: "Humankind may well stand at the beginning of a new kind of Copernican revolution—from a view centered around the nation-state to one in which the state system revolves around a commonality of a set of core values pertaining to human survival and solidarity." Violence between nation and nation does not further these aims. Global citizens have "to learn that the record of violence in achieving its objectives is a dismal one, that the use of violence often only invites greater counterviolence, and that the use of violence, however justified, may demolish the very goals and ideals that were sought, and create the mirror image of the injustice it sought to destroy."

As another participant observed, if the part keeps fighting for its ego at the expense of the whole, then the whole, including the part, may die. If the part were to acknowledge the value of the whole—a whole that cherishes the part—then both part and whole can live. This is Gaia's ecosystemic reality. "And this," she said, "is the true meaning of sacrifice. Sacrifice is not about suicide, a misguided self-betrayal for the sake of others, but about atonement, 'at-one-ment,' through the surrender of the defensive, separative ego, to a greater level of life."

Many people at the conference had referred to the role of the media, usually angrily. There was a strong feeling that the media had sold out to reactionary vested interests—to advertisers, to politicans in power, to newspaper barons with private agendas who want political power; the journalists had sold their birthright to the people with money who wanted the old aggressive status quo maintained, not revealed or altered. Tarzie Vittachi took on the task of clarifying the responsibility of journalists to the conference:

> What is the role of the communicators—we journalists of the mass media—in this crucial time in which the forces of destructive violence and the impulses of survival and development are moving side by side, though contrapuntally? Do we continue to make our customary, facile pleas that we are not participants in the drama being played out there and that our function is that of a

disinterested spectator holding up a mirror to society? If we do so, we must go all the way with a famous editor, the author of the following resonant words about the function of the free press, and I quote:

"The free press is the omnipresent open edge of the spirit of the people, the embodied confidence of a people in itself, the articulate bond that ties the individual with the state and the world, the incorporated culture which transfigures material struggles with intellectual ones, and idealizes its raw, material shape. It is the ruthless confession of a people to itself, and it is well known that the power of confession is redeeming. The free press is the intellectual mirror in which a people sees itself, and self-viewing is the first condition of wisdom."

Who wrote those lines? Lord Northcliffe? Lord Beaverbrook? A. J. Liebling? Joseph Pulitzer? Harold Evans when he was editing the *Times*? Rupert Murdoch? No. The editor of the Rheinische Zeitung, Karl Marx. I have quoted his words to suggest that there is a possibility for those engaged in our trade, whether we come from the West or East, North or South, to make common cause in the face of the enemy we have identified—the violence of war and the violence of poverty of body and soul—and to take a morally committed stance in our reporting of reality, just as some 150,000 physicians against nuclear war, who once pleaded scientific detachment, have abandoned that sterile attitude and have accepted the role of placing their professional skills in the service of peace.

Journalists have the right to ask searching questions, to probe, to have access to files, to analyze, to challenge, to speculate in print or on screen, in order that they might carry out their public duty: to report to the public all the public should know in order to make well-informed democratic decisions. A journalist is a servant of democracy. He or she has no special rights to collecting and disseminating information except in the performing of this democratic duty. The freedom of the press is a right, and a right is the power to fulfill a responsibility. Tarzie Vittachi put it like this:

I too cut my professional teeth in Fleet Street and became a fervent advocate of the freedom of the press and was vehement about my rights as a journalist. I still am. I abhor censorship of any kind and I have paid my union dues as an exile for my insistence, in the teeth of tyranny of the time in my own country, on writing what I believed to be the truth. But, as I observed overabundance, deer parks coexisting side by side with purulent slums, populations growing rapidly because too many children were dying from preventable causes so that parents were building insurance-size families as a hedge against the possibility of being left childless and their lines dying out, I began to be increasingly concerned not only with my rights but also with my responsibilities as a journalist. As this change was taking place in me, I asked myself ruefully as Ogden Nash had done:

> Am I just maturing late,
> or, simply, rotting early?

But that doubt has been resolved by the realisation that I owe my rights to the responsibilities of my craft.

How well have the communicators so far carried out their responsibilities of communicating to the public the problems confronting our planet? In the pub the other day, a man was holding forth about the greenhouse effect. It had to do with the ozone layer, he insisted. No, said a well-read and socially concerned young woman, it had to do with deforestation . . . hadn't it? Now that she was on the spot, she wasn't at all sure. Her friend said it might be, in a way. Or it might be to do with coal mining . . .

Carl Sagan, James Lovelock, we need you. We don't even have the basic facts straight, never mind the analysis. And we need journalists who will tell everyone what Sagan and Lovelock can tell us.

I have beside me an article from a large daily newspaper. It reads:

GREENHOUSES: FULL STORY REVEALED

Some people may be confused by alarming talk about The Greenhouse Effect, and how it threatens to end life as we know it on earth. Many do not read the small print. Greenhouses have never before been identified in the public imagination as a threat. On the contrary, people—especially small boys—have long been viewed as a threat to greenhouses. It would be unfortunate if any of the exemplary citizens who possess greenhouses—surely the nicest sort of people—felt they had to dismantle their haven for tomatoes in response to the crisis.

Perhaps one of the zealous new government ministers could put out an advisory leaflet on the subject. Greenhouses no threat to the world, says Minister.

This piece of feeble facetiousness is what the public was being offered in the summer of 1988 about the greenhouse effect. No wonder most of us are so ignorant even of life-and-death issues if our popular information sources keep us sedated with this kind of bland hooey.

A vague unease in the populace isn't enough to undermine inertia. We need a sharp shock—to sit on a pin to keep us from suffocating in an easy chair. Gregory Bateson once said: "My complaint with the kids I teach now is that they don't really believe anything enough to get the tension between the data and the hypothesis." Passionate engagement—where is it? It springs from clarity and commitment. The commitment is up to each individual. But clarity is the business of the communicator. How can the global citizen become engaged if communicators won't make clear what matters?

The tendency of most media communicators is to react like surprised children every time a disaster occurs and to blame easy scapegoats, like the weather, or the poor, or other people's wars. (Why are other people's wars always wasteful, while our own are essential?) Tarzie Vittachi reminded us that "the impoverishment of Africa" was not caused "just by unseasonable drought and brutish human conflict" as the majority of the press would have us believe, but also by more complex and far-reaching causes: the "market forces which are destroying the forests and the frail safety nets of subsistence agriculture that enabled the people of the Sahel to cope with drought for centuries."

But these complex and self-implicating processes are not publicized. Only the disaster at the end is reported, when tragedy is at its heights: "We report it only when the story breaks as a famine." And the half-truths go on: "We photograph children at the end of the scale of malnourishment, with their rickety limbs and distended bellies, and convey the impression that this is how an undernourished child looks. Ninety-eight percent of undernourishment is not like that: it is a furtive vampire disease invisible even to the mother's eye. We need to learn how to make the invisible visible by using our skills and our technology more professionally than we do."

When we meet other children from the poor world, rather small, perhaps, but smiling, we don't recognize them as malnourished. We "know" what a malnourished child looks like: dazed and distended. And we are surprised when an attack of measles or even a bout of flu is enough to carry these recently smiling children to their graves.

"We do not need a new world information order," Tarzie Vittachi continued,

> especially one that is sponsored by ministers of information who are in the business not of providing information but of suppressing it. But we do need a new information attitude, a new set of news values, and new training which enables us to make process reporting as interesting and vital as we make the daily events we report.
>
> Reporting process—finding answers to the questions "why" and "how"—is the inner dimension of journalism. "Who," "what," "where," and "when" are questions we have always asked. They deal with the outer aspects of human lives. We need both because life is not about either/or but about and/and. One without the other disables and impoverishes the mind.

Being a responsible journalist isn't simply a matter of reacting warm-heartedly to a tragedy. It is also a matter of being aware of the tragedy building up—aware because we have bothered to find out why the tragic process began. But that means being prepared to ask why all the way down the line—all the way until it leads back to our colleagues, our bosses, ourselves: our own part, moral or immoral, in the system that wreaks tragedy on the planet and the people who inhabit it. All of us in "the nonstarving classes," as Metropolitan Gregorios called us, communicators and noncommunicators alike, are part of the Earth's ecosystem. Communicators do not hold up a mirror; they too are inside the image.

Karl Marx had described the press as "the ruthless confession of a people to itself." In other words, journalists are that section of the people that analyze and articulate the psyche of the people; but they are still part of the people.

Communicators who imagine themselves to be separate from the main body of humanity distance themselves further and further, until eventually what happens to the mass of people no longer matters to them. They hide in trivia. An editor who rose to fame in the 1960s for blistering investigations of social injustice now edits the lowdown on where Princess Di does her shopping.

Safety through separation is an illusion. Since communicators are part of Gaia, whether they like it or not, their attempt to cut themselves off has a fragmenting, destructive effect on the whole. They are a strand in the web—and when they try to unpick one strand and pull it away, the whole web is pulled awry. If turning aside from tragedy is their response to it, then not only have journalists failed to report responsibly on human misery, they have made an active contribution to it. The failure to report thoroughly, process as well as event, after tragedy strikes is the second stage of journalists' betrayal; the first is maintaining the self-delusion that they can stand as a group apart.

It is a scientific commonplace now that the observer of an experiment always affects the result of the experiment. There is no objective place an observer can stand; there is nowhere that is outside the experiment. The observer, so to speak, is always in the test tube.

If we do not recognize the Heisenberg principle then we do not take responsibility for our part in the result of the experiment. We imagine that the result is an objective truth and that we merely observed it. Our objective truth, therefore, is necessarily false, both because it is partial and because we have denied its partiality. If we choose to see ourselves as merely observers we cannot tell the truth. And yet most of us every day do insist that what we see is the truth. One consequence of this denial is very serious. We perpetuate the myth that there is a single truth, outside us, to tell. We accept that we may make the odd mistake with the detail or have a bit of bias, but basically we still believe that there is a single truth of which we have a good, if not perfect, grasp.

This faith in objectivity is a habit of thought that has spread powerfully across the world. But it is not universal. Like Soedjatmoko, who wanted students to understand that there are "multiple ways of perceiving and expressing truth," Professor Raimundo Panikkar's was a voice that spoke at the conference in praise of a complex vision of many simultaneous truths. He is a professor of philosophy, as elegant and precise as the fine philosophical distinctions he likes to make.

On Thursday evening, the final evening of the conference, in my student room overlooking Peckwater Quad, he held forth to a small group of us, who were alternately baffled and illuminated by his words. He was mercurial, dramatic, one moment crouching on the floor and speaking in a soft growl so that we had to strain to hear and the next throwing his arms open wide and speaking fast and high . . . It was quite a performance, much admired by us all.

Professor Panikkar objected powerfully to the adoration of the picture of the Earth taken from space. "We have all been mesmerized to say that this is the world," he said crushingly. "To have waited fifty thousand years to know what is the Earth! In 1054 you had the most marvelous description of the Earth. It is three thousand times more beautiful, more telling—without having the need of a snap!"

Why did he object so strenuously to this "snap"? It was an example, he felt, of a monocultural view—a technological view, by which we had all been seduced. We were so transfixed by this way of seeing, so dependent on it, that we didn't even realize any more that it was only one way of seeing. We had caved in and come to imagine that what we saw through this view was the truth, rather than one view of the truth—like looking through a window, he said, and imagining we were looking directly at what we saw, because we had forgotten that the glass is there, filtering our vision.

Not only was he exasperated with us for being naive enough

to forget that we were looking through a filter, he also didn't have much regard for the quality of this particular filter.

> Science and technology, what I call the technological complex, has backfired, to say the least. It does not deliver the goods. We have been living with this kind of projection into the future for centuries. I am convinced that the modern projection of Western science and technology is perverse, in the theological sense of "perversion," the opposite of "conversion"—the fragmentation of knowledge. Which brings about what we have today—the fragmentation of the world. The world is fragmented, and we assume that by putting together all the pieces of the puzzle, we will get the whole. This is again wrong; the whole is not the sum total of the parts. The more we investigate, the more we follow the Cartesian rule, the less we find the truth. The more complicated, the more sophisticated, and the more distanced we are from anything.

So we shouldn't wait for Western science, with its fragmenting, analytic, objective culture, to prove to us what is true? "I am saying that reality is not totally intelligible. That truth itself is pluralistic. There are many truths. There is a mystery which we cannot grasp beyond single or plural. That is why I challenge the meteorological approach of the conference." At least, this is what I understood Professor Panikkar to say; I was painfully aware of the limitations of my understanding when he pressed against its boundaries, and I often found him, like truth, to be fascinating but mysterious.

What I could readily see was that holding a hardened monoview makes us intolerant; for if I regard the truth that I see as the truth—and I know myself to be sincere in my looking—then I must conclude that your truth must be faulty. I will therefore be inclined try to persuade you (for your own good, of course) that you are wrong and I am right. Professor Panikkar had said: "The word *convince* comes from the idea of conquering—see, *con-vince*, and *vincere* means 'to conquer.' Instead of *understand*—to 'stand under' this new idea."

Even the idea of persuading someone else is a subtle form of

117

violence; you are overcoming or conquering someone else's idea
with your own. It is a very different approach to offer your point
of view, which others may, if they wish, come and stand under,
as if under a beam of sunlight or a cleansing rain cloud. This
"under-standing" was very much in line with what I had learned
from Rachel Pinney about listening rather than arguing; and also
from the Dalai Lama, when he invited us to take what we agreed
with from his speech and implement it in our own lives, but
otherwise to forget it.

The conference as a whole, whatever the professor's reservations, had struck me as being like this: a receptacle that held many
truths, from which we could each draw our own synthesis, rather
than a single view that the organizers had imposed on us from
start to finish. This approach seemed to me to be reflected delicately (and presumably quite unconsciously) in the gifts given out
at the end of the conference to the main contributors. The speakers, the sponsors, and various others who had helped put the
conference together, were each given a large, engraved, glass
goblet, very like a grail. And the grail, as in the myth of the Holy
Grail, has been understood by psychologists to be an archetypal
symbol of synthesis and wholeness.

In the grail myth, the land is parched and dying while it is
ruled only by the king, the patriarch, the dominant masculine
principle; the king himself is dying, bloodless, from a wound,
along with his kingdom. Only when this dominating one-sided-
ness is balanced and completed by the inclusion of the feminine
principle (the grail brims with blood like a womb in Parsifal's
vision at the start of the quest, to point him in the direction of
what's missing)—in other words, only when masculine and feminine principles, yin and yang, come together in synthesis and
wholeness—is there healing for the sterile land.

But where wholeness isn't the aim, we have polarization and
conflict. There arises a competition where we each try to prove
that our truth is *the* truth. During this competition, I will defend
my truth in every way, finding evidence to support it, suppress-
ing—thinkingly or not—evidence that contradicts it; and I will find
ways to diminish your view. For, insofar as my identity is depend-

ent on my beliefs seeming well founded, then if I am proved to be wrong, I am shaken in the foundations of my being.

This, indeed, is what the media usually help us do. With each gulp of news, our "objective" reporters chew down the complexity they receive, simplify it to the level of their prejudices, and then amplify their prejudices in print. Their loyal readers buy whichever prejudices correspond with their own, denouncing the other versions as written by liars. Thus do we shore up our threatened sense of identity: not by thinking but by avoiding fresh thought. As Tolstoy wrote in *Anna Karenina*, Stepan Arkadyevitch always read the same kind of newspaper, and "he enjoyed it just as much as a cigar after dinner, because of the mistiness with which it enveloped his mind."

Conflict is the media's fast food. At journalism school, confessed my brother, if the student journalists were short of a story—they usually had to find half a dozen stories by lunchtime—they soon learned that the fastest way to manufacture it was by exploiting the polarization built in to our present habits of thought and behavior. First they would phone up, say, the local conservative councilor and ask him his views on some issue; then they would phone up a more liberal councilor and ask him if the opposition agreed with the conservative's view. "Of course not!" would be the certain reply. A dramatic story would appear in the next news bulletin: "Conflict at the Council Chambers."

It was grimly amusing to note the same manufacturing of conflict in some of the media coverage of the conference itself. The Archbishop of Canterbury's measured, carefully distanced speech was reported by London's *Daily Express* newspaper under the headline "Runcie in Politics Row." Anything less like a row would be hard to imagine.

Not amusing at all was the report of the conference in the *Daily Telegraph*. Written in a chummy, smug style, sprinkled with cinema verité details to persuade you that the reporter had actually been present, it told how Mother Teresa was "fingering her rosary," for instance—a fairly safe shot. But the reporter's bluff was called when he told us that James Grant "spoke movingly of the problems of poverty." James Grant wasn't at the conference—he was attending his wife's funeral in New York.

The false reality continued, getting grimmer. Accompanying

the story was a large close-up photograph of Metropolitan Gregorios, a learned and complex man who speaks several languages
more eloquently than most of us speak one. The Metropolitan was
photographed with his eyes closed. But the caption didn't interpret
this as a possible sign of prayer, or reflection, or even weariness. It
made the assumption that it was a sign of ignorance: "For one
delegate," it said, "something was lost in the translation." Presumably because the Metropolitan has a brown face, the caption writer,
and all the editors and subeditors who passed the caption, felt able
to invite the readers to collude with them in the outrageous
assumption that the poor man just couldn't understand English.

Tarzie Vittachi tried to remain optimistic about journalists. He
said:

> There is more awareness now of the danger of
> reporting the world in nineteenth-century stereotypes.
> A hundred years ago, Henry M. Stanley, an American
> journalist, was sent to Africa to look for an Englishman
> "lost" in the jungles of Tanganyika—now called Tanza-
> nia. It was a circulation stunt. . . . On his way back, he
> was invited by the Manchester Chamber of Commerce
> to address them. In that remarkable speech there are a
> few lines which have embossed themselves on my mem-
> ory rolls:
>
> "There are fifty million of people beyond the gate-
> way to the Congo, and the cotton spinners of Manches-
> ter are waiting to clothe them. Birmingham foundries
> are glowing with the red metal that will presently be
> made into ironwork for them, and the trinkets shall
> adorn those dusky bosoms. And the ministers of Christ
> are zealous to bring them, the poor benighted heathen,
> into the Christian fold."
>
> There we are. Africans who, as far as we know,
> were the first to evolve from ape to man, seen as
> primitive, passive, inarticulate creatures, waiting for the
> boons of empire to redeem them from barbarism. Evi-
> dently they had no culture, no history of their own.
> They are seen through the prefocused lenses of coloni-
> alism, which take a zoological view of all dark strangers.

But, I say to myself, that was a hundred years ago. . . . How could Stanley have thought otherwise? But, again, when one sees that same zoological viewpoint existing in the media today, there is cause for alarm.

What does he see as the purpose of real journalism? "Metanoia, a true change of heart and mind," he says. "Information that does not transform is just gossip."

11 *The Solution is the Problem*

After the final no there comes a yes.
And on that yes the future world depends.
                    WALLACE STEVENS

T HORNTON Bradshaw, head of the MacArthur Foundation, was the last of the conference's keynote speakers, and he began on a positive note: "The world is rapidly becoming one global village, driven by scientific advances and economic necessities. For the first time in human history, we can foresee food for all, shelter for all, health for all, and beyond that a rising standard of living for all." But his anxieties followed swiftly:

> And yet, despite that glowing possibility, many people are unhappy about prospects for the future. They believe that given the tools of science and technology we will create a world well stocked with goods but poorly stocked with human happiness. They believe that the price of a global village is the loss of a sense of belonging. They believe we will have to live in a global village without the warmth, the human relations, the familiar territory, the moral markings of the people's villages of our youth. They believe the price is too high.

He was voicing a concern we had all felt, that global unity could equal a massive homogeneity. As the Archbishop of Canterbury had said, no one wanted a blancmange. But as the conference had proceeded, we had come to see that we could have both unity and diversity; we could feel ourselves to be members of one planet, while celebrating our differences and belonging to the tribal groups in which we felt at home. We just had to take care not to be so trapped inside our differences that we could never see beyond

122

them; we needed to feel free enough to see our neighbor on the other side of the ocean just as compassionately as the neighbor on the other side of the street.

"We businessmen are part of the problem," he acknowledged. "We businessmen have done more to create this new interdependent world than any other group." He offered the example of people around the world watching the American TV program *Dallas* as an example of a dismaying sort of unity: a thin film of commercialism that had little to do with the kind of interdependence we had been valuing at the conference.

What Thornton Bradshaw feared—as we all do—was the imposition of a monoculture, a giant octopus sprawling over a living diversity. True interdependence was about having the chance and the courage to taste many flavors, not about smothering everything in chemical flavorings so that the contents of a plastic packet taste the same in Chattanooga or China. Interdependence was about all of us having the opportunity to enjoy multiplicity—as indeed we were doing at the conference, when we offered the insights that came from our different religions or ways of life—not about a bland uniformity.

Fortunately for us all, this film of artificially sweetened blancmange has not yet turned the world into as homogeneous a global village as Mr. Bradshaw feared it might. Professor Panikkar, for one, did not believe in its existence.

If this metaphorical village consists of one hundred families, said the professor, then some ninety families do not speak English, and sixty-five cannot read. Some eighty families have no members who have flown on airplanes, and seventy have no drinking water at home.

About sixty families occupy 10 percent of the village, while just seven families own 60 percent of the land. Seven families also consume 80 percent of all available energy, and only one family has a university education. And the inequities are getting worse.

What kind of a village could this be, where there are seven mansions and an airport on one side, and no drinking water at home on the other? Community feelings in this village are obviously few and patchy. The world is not yet a global village—not in the sense that it needs to be.

Thornton Bradshaw quoted Donne's famous lines: "No man

is an island, entire of itself; every man is a piece of the continent, a part of the main; if a clod be washed away by the sea, Europe is the less . . . any man's death diminishes me, because I am involved in mankind." Clearly, justice demands that we feel solidarity, as Donne did, in order that we encourage the changes that will bring clean water to every villager. And when we talk of interconnectedness, we must be careful not to confuse the human need for a "clean water culture" with the commercial push for a Coca-Cola culture.

Bradshaw also drew attention to the international problem with distributing wealth. The cynical free-marketeering of Adam Smith and David Ricardo, he said, was still dominant: "the same economic concept of seeking the lowest cost factors of production [means that] the girls of Taiwan are paid a dollar sixty-five an hour, the girls of Indiana about fifteen dollars an hour." And a girl in Morocco may be paid only fifteen cents an hour, for weaving a carpet that sells for thousands of dollars in New York.

His talk confirmed to me a principle I had learned before: that genuine interdependence can operate only between people who stand in positions of equal power and can demand equal rights; otherwise, it merely institutionalizes economic exploitation. Commercial cooperation around the world must be linked with political and economic equality. It also reminded me that, because of the extreme inequality of our times, people who are indifferent to a sense of the larger human family can exploit the poor with ease. They need to feel more planetary solidarity, like Donne: diminished by every unnecessary death, wherever in the world that death occurs. We must know without a doubt that every child who dies of malnourishment because his mother was paid at the lowest possible rate diminishes us; we must feel the grief of that diminishment in our blood and bones.

Father Jean-Claude Lavigne, an economist specializing in North-South interdependence, was one of the small group that gathered on the final evening of the conference in my room for a last pause for reflection on the issues raised by the conference before we parted on Friday morning. I asked him why he had chosen to specialize in the North-South issue.

Father Lavigne: When I studied in the North, I stayed within the cultural mind-sets and assumptions of the North; it was only when I traveled in Asia, in India, that I realized there were many other ways to see. There was a kind of transfer of technology for me from South to North, in the new understanding I gained.

For example, in the North, one thinks of employment in terms of jobs; and what we count as a job is something dogmatically defined. If you want to go through the economic crisis, we have to change this. There can be no salaried job for everyone, this is impossible, it's a myth. Full employment is a myth of the 1960s.

In the South, you see that revenue is the most important thing. So I think my fight is not to provide jobs but revenue and activity. When you go to the South, you see flexibility there—you yourself can build a way of living, a way of earning revenue; create the job.

I don't say that the South has the truth, no, but it gave me new experiences—it was not a matter of theory. I received some fresh insight, new questions I wanted to ask in my country, in my culture. My experience can be useful as questions—not as solutions.

Q: Experiences of shaking the old mindsets, so there is room to rethink?

Father Lavigne: To rethink together. Because I think that the cooperation we have to make with the South is like that. We have to share first our failure.

Q: Our failure? Isn't cooperation about sharing our successes—offering our knowledge, our solutions?

Father Lavigne: We have made failure in the matter of growth, in the way we deal with the energy problem, with pollution. I can be truthful if I share with the people how I fail—and how they fail—and together we can overcome the failure.

I think it is most important to not show off—"I am a success!"—and so on. I am a failure, so I have to analyze why; and you also have failed; so we must think together, how can we manage to overcome this failure, both of us? It is a mature approach to overcome the problems we face.

Q: So there are two conventional alternatives: one is the competitive, egoist approach, which involves you, as the protagonist, suggesting, "I am a complete success." In this approach, if you don't know something, you feel very insecure and you cover

125

up your ignorance. Then there is another approach, which is the cooperative approach, but even there you have to have at least part of the answer. Here, I say that I have an answer, you have an answer, we will share it and get a bigger, better answer. But we still have to have an answer to share. What you are saying is something else again.

Father Lavigne: Yes, postcrisis, no answer at all.

Q: Do you mean that not knowing the answer is a way of letting go the narrowness of old solutions; we need to see the act of letting go known solutions as valuable in itself, as an important part of the process of transcending the past? Then maybe something genuinely new can emerge from the cooperation, not just a compromise, or an amalgamation of old ideas, but something really fresh.

Father Lavigne: I think so. But to be like that, you need to trust the other people who are in front of you. It means you recognize that the other has culture, has knowledge and so on, just as you have. We don't show off, destroy other people. We share failure: it is a positive way.

Q: So are we talking about fellowship, you and me against the world—or, at least, against the world's problems? We're thinking about the quality, and equality, of our relationship.

Father Lavigne: We think economy is only about production of materials, of goods. But that is a very small part of economy. You have to look also at distribution, at the distribution of wealth, and consumption. Now, in the new economics, you have to look at what is your motivation, what is your choice, what is your criteria of choice—that is, ethics. How can we deal with others? What relation do we have with others? Production, distribution, and consumption is something between you and the other.

Q: So the relationship between us and other people is crucial. The way we organize concrete factors like production, distribution, and consumption expresses this inner relationship—the manifestation of whether our relationship is competitive, or whether it expresses solidarity; for example, if we don't really care what apartheid does to people then we can continue to have economic dealings with the government of South Africa; but if we feel solidarity with the black people there, we will consider what each deal does to them.

Father Lavigne: When you use the word *solidarity* it means a little bit more than listening to each other. [He hesitated a second, and then began again, very seriously.] I can speak in a mystic way? Solidarity is when someone enters your life, and you cannot expel him out of your life. It is not only sharing. Sharing is one thing. Yes, it is good, it is important. But temporary. Sometimes you share. Solidarity is something more. It means that you cannot decide, make choices—political choices and so on—without thinking of him. He is part of your life, he is part of you.

Q: Like . . . the difference between giving charity, loose change, to a stranger, and not being able to eat the plate of food in front of me if it means my child has none? Because she is part of my life.

Father Lavigne: She is part of your life; so solidarity is like that. And our North/South approach is also like that.

Q: Not "them," those strangers over there, that "we" are being charitable to, but we are all part of each others' lives.

Father Lavigne: So in this conference we make a path. We take the first steps—we know each other, we have discovered that we have so many good ideas together. The next step will be when these new relationships, new insights, become part of my decision, part of my choice.

I make a decision, let us say an investment decision, or a political decision. When the Other is a part of my choice, then in the moment I choose something, he is there. When I buy a share, I think who is going to be the beneficiary. When I make a choice, do I give to the Other a chance to exist. . . .

It is a mystical way, I know. But I think we have to go like that. Not just to be idealistic—but the Other has to be a part of your life. We have to know the Other, not to invent the Other. The best way to avoid the Other is to invent the Other.

Q: How do we invent the Other?

Father Lavigne (laughing): So: "Oh, I live in the North, so I am bad, egoistic, and every one in the South is so nice"—it is the best way to avoid them.

Q: Inverted racism. Because it is a fantasy, a pretence.

Father Lavigne: Pornographic poverty is the same. It is the best way to avoid poor people—to make them different. To see them as "so nice, so lively, so communitary."

127

Q: I admit I become very irritated when people say things like: "Since you are black you must be very musical." It is really racist, although it is presented as if it were a compliment.

Father Lavigne (enjoying himself): Or: "So convivial, so friendly, so nice." It is one way to avoid the people.

Q: Then they are just a projection of your own; you are not really seeing them as real people at all.

Father Lavigne: And in order to overcome that, you have to make analysis—so someone can be the Other to you. You have to analyze what he thinks, what is his limit, what is his power advantage, and so on. You have to analyze this, because when you see clearly he becomes the true Other.

So this conference is something like that—we tried to understand who is the real Other; it means seeing what is my difference from him, what is my similarity, and so on. To really see, without inventing how beautiful he is, how nice the native culture is, how nice the Hopi is—it *is* nice, but I have to understand what it is.

Q: Gramsci said you must have an optimistic heart and a pessimistic head. Is it a little like that, having a head that is very critical and always making sure what you see is not a fantasy, and a heart that is open and ready to accept and explore and trust; to have some faith and some generosity?

Father Lavigne: But both . . . otherwise you invent the Other, and you don't understand what he says to you. You protect yourself by putting him in a beautiful golden carapace.

We had this conversation late on Thursday evening. On Friday morning, I woke up with a deep ache. It was the last day of the conference, and I was very sad it was over. But the ache was more particular than that.

As usual, I found Father Lavigne in the dining hall, over the toast and marmalade. Luckily, he had a spare seat beside him. "I've woken up with this awful pain," I said. "And I've been trying to work out what it is. I've just realized: after the conversation last night, my husband and I would really like you to come home with us."

Father Lavigne started to laugh.

"Really," I said. "We can't bear the thought of you going back to France and not being part of our family any more."

128

"Ah," he said. "So . . . now you know what solidarity is."

I talked to Wilfrid Grenville-Grey, one of the conference organizers, about the value of failure. It had been a revelation for me, addicted as I had always been to perfection. "If I am conscious of my failure," I explained, as much to myself as to him, "then I am not trying to dominate the other with my solution, my answer. Nor is he trying to dominate me, if he also values his failure. We are both interested only in solving the problem before us. Our egos are not involved, because we are not attached to our solutions—we have no adequate solutions, when we recognize that what we have are failures.

"Well, the first problem we decided we had to solve is peace, how to find peace instead of being in conflict with each other. And then we realized, if we are sitting beside each other, trying to find peace together, we are already at peace! Peace is here."

In response, Wilfrid, as always, pulled out a quotation from his never-ending supply: "There is no way to peace. Peace is the way."

Father Lavigne's phrase "inventing the Other" also reverberated in my mind; it reminded me of the references several speakers, among them Manuel Ulloa and Soedjatmoko, had made about the difficulties caused by people being divided inside themselves. When we deny the parts we are ashamed or afraid of and project those parts onto other people, we see these other people wrapped in an illusory veil of our projections; we invent them.

How were we to see people more clearly, undistorted by the veil of our illusions? Presumably we needed to acknowledge those projections, take them back and recognize them as parts of our own selves. Then we would become more rounded and complete in ourselves, less divided, and with fewer illusions about ourselves and others. We would be in a position to be more responsive to others, if we were not pretending to be different from who we are—or pretending that others are different from who they are.

Dr. Ariyaratne said something that made these several pieces fall into place for me.

> Spirituality is basically how an individual relates to himself or herself. The person whose objective is his

own awakening, in the sense of purification of his mind, relates himself better to other individuals . . . and the kind of relationship he will establish with other human beings will be nonexploitative, uncompetitive, more co-operative, and more affectionate. That is a kind of lifting up of the moral relationships in society.

Today that relationship is no longer there. Those who are privileged will try to exploit others by their power or their will. So spiritual and moral renewal is the second kind of awakening we need for our world [after we understand] natural laws. And then political and economic arrangements should be based on these two. If we can bring that dimension to the present-day world, we can think of a better future, a more peaceful world, a happier community.

I have for some time been finding it harder and harder to believe in the sort of leaders who preach equality and justice in public but bully their spouse and children at home. The values people live by spontaneously are the ones that count, not the ones they pontificate about.

Now it seemed that the concept of *home* was to be taken to an even deeper level: *home* was our inner home, the place our own selves resided within us. If that home was divided, one part dominating and denying the value of the other, or even noisily drowning out the evidence of the other's existence, how could we be wholesome in our attitudes to the rest of our world?

12 Past, Present, and Future

> There is an impulse still within the human breast
> to unify and sanctify the total natural world—of
> which we are.
>
> GREGORY BATESON

THE experience of the conference suggested that we can at least take one first, conscious step in the process towards metanoia. That step is to recognize on just how narrow a base we build our present beliefs and our vision of future possibilities—and therefore to be willing to look beyond this narrow base. It tends to be little more than an extension of the beliefs and hopes on which we have relied in the past.

We have seen the power of technology, for instance, to make some lives prosperous and comfortable in the past—and so we have relied on technology to make our lives more comfortable also in the future. But now we fall into despair, because it seems that our faith has been betrayed. Technology is not going to save us by some scientific miracles: the "green revolution" has not fed the starving; medical miracles have not saved a quarter of a million children dying every week. On the contrary, technology seems to be magnifying the dangers. The greenhouse effect has already started to rearrange our weather patterns. "Red sky at night" used to mean "shepherd's delight"—a sunny morning next day. Now, weather experts fear, red skies may only mean that the sky is being painted over with too much carbon dioxide.

And what about our other old answers? We have habitually relied on our parents, or our political leaders, or our spiritual leaders—whoever has been a powerful authority in our lives—to tell us what to do. But humanity has now come to the brink of death and not one of our authority figures from the past seems

131

able to save us. Our parents are as lost as we are, in a runaway world. Our spiritual and political leaders have not saved us from the threat of mass death by war. Instead, we see the world continuing to stride toward disaster.

With a loss of faith in our old answers, and in the people who gave us our answers in times past, many of us find ourselves afraid and hopeless. Not only is the world outwardly, ecologically, in danger, but we know ourselves to be in internal, psychic danger as well, as the foundations of our inner certainties crumble. Yeats' lines, "Things fall apart—the center cannot hold," are quoted more and more often. That center is within ourselves.

We are suffering an existential crisis: a crisis of meaninglessness. Outer suffering is made bearable by a deep inner conviction in there being meaning in that suffering. Prisoners of conscience will endure torture and survive because of their belief in a better way that can and will arise in the near future. But when that conviction fails, when hope fails, then meaning fails, and the will to endure fails also.

When individuals hit crises of meaning like this, as therapist Chris Robertson said to me after the conference, they move towards suicide. And when the whole planet hits such a crisis, we have the danger of mass suicide. This is what we are facing now. A mass suicide—sometimes expressed as a silent giving up, sometimes as a violent cry of pain. The question facing us now is, Where in the world can we find a source of realistic hope instead of realistic despair? Where are we to find new springs of meaning and purpose? In whom can we put our trust?

To let go old certainties is a painful business: they are a major part of our identity. Some of us continue to hang on to these certainties like grim death, even when we know them to be invalid. Others take alternative pain-avoidance escape routes (from drug addiction to shopping addiction). Some are willing to face the painful process of letting go the narrow certainties of the past and to take the risk of seeing what then emerges into view. This was what, it seemed to me, we had been trying out at Oxford. We had been willing to let go our certainties a little way and to see what else, if anything, there was to be seen at the conference. And what we had seen was not so much an answer, in the sense of tangible practicalities, but an experience of empathy and trust. If we could genuinely trust ourselves and each other, then the options available to us as we work out our practical solutions will be quite different—as the nuclear disarmament talks have shown.

One participant offered a personal example of widening options:

> I grazed past suicide several years ago after the loss of my husband; most of the meaning in my life I had placed in sharing my life with him. What kept me from falling off the edge was the life I saw in my small children. This seemed to me to have incontrovertible value. The children were my raison d'etre, until new aspects of my life surfaced as also having meaning. Now I have no wish to die—I am hungry for life.
>
> But the important point here is that these other "containers of meaning" I now enjoy were always there: I just couldn't see them while I was busy looking inside the single box, now terrifyingly empty, where I had placed most of the meaning I saw. The turning point came when I stopped hopelessly looking inside the empty box and was finally prepared to look elsewhere. Where I looked was at myself.
>
> I saw that I had always kept myself very small, kept my possibilities very narrow, in order to stay within the framework of my old belief. As a woman, I believed I had to look weak and to lean on my husband, even though I knew in my heart I was strong. When that old narrow framework was gone, I had the choice whether to stay small and despairing or to grow into a larger framework that actually expressed my true self better. It seemed to me at first that my loss had deprived me of meaning; instead it had presented me with the opportunity to stop betraying myself by pretending to be smaller than I was.

We needed to look for the future not in the narrow certainties of the past but in the crises and uncertainties of an expanded present; the miraculous insights lay not somewhere in the future but in the experience of now. At the conference itself we had experienced, from time to time, these mysterious flashes of solidarity, of communion in the midst of diversity, of being on the same side. The experience of trust and solidarity was not an idealist's promise for the future: it was a living reality in the present.

It belonged to the future only in one sense: it could provide a model for the future that was more hopeful than the old divisive one that led us inexorably to conflict and death. Not that the future will look exactly like this model of solidarity—the one thing we can predict about the future is that it will never be as we expect—but it will give us a light to follow now. We will have to wait and see where it will lead us in time.

We could derive hope also from the thought that existential crises are not new—at least on a personal level, though it may be a new planetary experience. It is a simple fact that virtually every adult, by the time they are forty or fifty, has gone through at least one period in their lives when they have hovered on the edge of despair, coming close to suicide, because of a sense of despairing meaninglessness. And yet the vast majority of us do not kill ourselves. We come through our crises more truly ourselves than we went into them and are glad, after all, that we made the choices necessary to survive.

In planetary terms, too, we have now been presented with an opportunity, as Princess Elizabeth put it, "to be our true selves" and not betray ourselves any more by being smaller than we are. Keeping ourselves locked up in the old confines of nation-states, as political leaders in the past have encouraged us to, invites war; at the conference, there was a call instead to recognize ourselves in a new, larger frame of cooperation between global citizens that was perceived at the conference as a truer delineation of the human being. The picture of the Earth from space was constantly called upon to prove the truth of this new global perception.

The Earth has always looked like this: one sphere. It is not a new reality in fact. And yet perceiving the wholeness of the Earth is a new reality of perception. The point was not, it seemed to me, that the astronauts' seeing the Earth as a whole made people see the Earth differently, as has been claimed; rather, it could be that by the time the astronauts took the picture, the citizens of the Earth were in any case beginning to need an image that expressed their growing sense of planetarism. The picture was a useful image to encapsulate the half-conscious understanding that was, in any case, evolving and beginning to emerge.

Apart from the call to become planetarists, in a political and spiritual ecumenism, other suggestions from the participants revealed a larger, planet-sized vision kicking its way into lusty life at the conference. There was a call from Father Berry for the UN's Charter for Nature (which most of us had never even heard of till then) to be recognized and implemented in the form of local charters for nature. There was a call also for the establishment of a "global commons," whose international trustees would ensure that the ecological resources of the planet would be protected for the good of all humankind's future generations. There was a suggestion that there should be a global income tax, in the form of a direct tax paid by individuals to the UN, which would then be distributed to the poorer citizens of the world. At present, we were reminded, governments do make a contribution to the UN on our behalf—but since this contribution is so indirect (and tiny), how many of us even realize that the payment is made? There was acknowledgement, too, that planetarist agreements at the conference were not enough. As Metropolitan Gregorios said, political strategies must now follow; governmental policies must be put into effect that ensure the intentions are translated into fact.

But action follows vision; energy follows thought. We cannot diminish the importance at the conference of this recognition of a new planet-sized context—that is the key shift. It is a shift of scale and scope, not only in geographical size but in cultural complexity. And the value given to the bigger meaning, for once, does not obliterate the value given to individual empowerment.

On the contrary, both individual and collective levels, both the one and the many, are honored together. The vision is plural—unity includes diversity, through a recognition of the two levels of community to which each of us belongs, the home community, which satisfies our personal, "solar plexus" need to belong, and the planetary community, which answers our longing to encompass all we can understand and love.

And the vision is flexible not only in spatial terms, stretching to encompass all living cultures, but also in temporal terms; whatever truth we come to understand now will in its turn become a construction that is too narrow and will have to be discarded.

135

How marvelous to look forward to the day when globalism will be too narrow a concept. What will we be urged towards next? Solar systemism? Galaxism?

Father Tom Berry was one of the delegates for whom planetarism probably already seemed too narrow. "The universe," he said,

> is an enormous psychic-spiritual reality. The [mechanistic descriptions of the universe] have left out the fact that the story of the universe is the story of an emergent consciousness process. All things share in this, though at certain levels this is minimal in its expression. . . . We ourselves, humans, are not so much part of the universe, not so much a being *in* the universe as a mode of being *of* the universe. We are that being in whom the universe reflects on, and celebrates, itself. It's not that we are doing it; the universe is reflecting on and celebrating itself. That's the purpose of life—celebration.

Any visions we come up with concerning the meaning and purpose of life, even those as joyful as Tom Berry's, we must continue to recognize as temporary and partial solutions, useful for the time being but liable to change, and open to being enriched by others. When we admit these limits to knowing the answer—indeed, when we acknowledge our inability ever to know the whole answer about the Earth and humankind's place in it—then we begin the process of freeing the space for wisdom.

Seeing this process of letting go, of releasing our grip on our familiar sectarian identities to the spirit of a previously unknown planetary community—seeing it actually beginning to happen in a large, disparate group like this was what made the conference special for me. It made the week a creative experience, not just a time and place where one gathered a mass of papers with disparate opinions jostling on them. The meaning of the conference wasn't on bits of paper; it was in the experience of the conference's spirit. We hadn't merely been told the result of a successful experiment; we had become aware that we were part of it.

I asked Dr. Velikhov what his message from the conference would be to people outside. He thought a moment and said: "Never ask for whom the bell tolls." That was exactly the point. We were in this together; after the experience of the Oxford conference we could never forget that. The importance of seeing our unavoidable inclusion within the experiment was one of the key insights for me. Failure to perceive ourselves as included in the experiment had led us to see truth as separate and colonizable; and in that same false mental set, we had seen the Earth as separate and colonizable too. It has been a near-fatal mistake.

Of course people had reservations about the conference. The organizers asked to hear about them in a questionnaire whose answers were collated and redistributed.

Some people were alarmed by the thought of staying in student rooms and preferred Oxford's best hotel. Others found even the college setting unnecessarily plush. John Taylor of the World Council of Churches, a gentle, courteous man, spoke of "a World Conference on Religion and Peace that had been held in a developing country in a teacher training college outside a village. We lived simply. Partway through the conference the water ran out and we experienced what it was like to live in a country where this happens. It captured the imagination of the participants." Suddenly they were involved not intellectually but experientially in the difficulties they had been talking about. "In no time at all, a fund with half a million dollars had been set up for a water project."

Rowan Williams, canon of Christ Church, like Professor Panikkar, objected to the image of the Earth from space dominating the conference hall every day: "We could have had a different image each day—a mandala, for example. . . . I am very conscious of the technological framework within which we meet. My fantasy would be to have a conference where people did their own cooking and chatted over the washing up." It was over the washing up that people said the things that really mattered to them.

The lack of interstice time was a problem. The program was so packed with talks and meetings that it was difficult to find enough time to "just be," either by oneself or with others. It was a major difficulty for me, trying to talk to as many people informally as I could in such short time in order to get a sense of their experience of the conference. Four and a half days, with meetings or entertainments scheduled from nine in the morning till late in the evening, sometimes till midnight, didn't leave time to get to know more than a fraction of the people I wanted to meet.

There were other worries. Some found the midweek banquet at Blenheim Palace in excruciating taste. Without doubt it was meant charmingly, and thus did we try to accept it. The hosts were offering to their illustrious guests with unstinting generosity the best that they felt the host country could offer. But to many of us it seemed painfully inappropriate when we had been discussing stripping the Earth and failing to feed the hungry. While the Reverend C. T. Vivian, friend of the late Dr. Martin Luther King, Jr., was saying grace, thanking the Almighty for "this simple food" (surely with a twinkle in his eye), I opened mine to see every plate set with a ramekin smothered in caviar.

Conversation with the guest on my left, Dr. Ariyaratne, was almost impossible, drowned out by the blaring of a vast and hideous organ. Squeezed uncomfortably into fancy clothes for the occasion, deafened by the music, queasy on the ultrarich food, uneasy at being served by young women dressed like Victorian parlor maids who had never heard of votes for women, I longed to continue the conversation with Ari peacefully under a tree on a village green. Giving up the kind of luxury we were being bombarded with would have been no sacrifice at all.

In a blessed lull in the organ playing, Ari told us the story of a very rich man who had asked him to visit him at his home. The dinner table had been laid for two, each of the plates guarded on either side by serried ranks of silverware. The rich man had invited Ari over to talk about world hunger. It concerned him deeply. What could he do to help? Ari said, "This." And leaning forward, he cleared away four-fifths of the spoons and forks and knives.

We all laughed at the story. But the sad thing was, Ari said, the rich man hadn't understood at all what he meant.

The conference ended with a declaration put together by a committee and drafted by Kusumita Pedersen. The first version was read out to the conference by Karan Singh and presented by Mavis Gilmour. There were some reservations among the participants, many but not all of which were incorporated into a revised version. One reservation came from James Lovelock. He objected to the Earth being portrayed as fragile. Gaia, he reminded us, was tough. It was we who were at risk.

And there were reservations, especially from Metropolitan

Antonio of Transylvania and from Canon Rowan Williams, about the weakness of the statements about justice for the poor. During the coffee break the metropolitan said that to solve the conflicts between the rich and the poor, we needed "a new economic order, peacefully realized—people in power to solve the problems, not just to hide them." He wanted our ideas to be given the force of law. A "common moral order" should be enshrined in treaties that were respected, based on common moral values like the sanctity of life. "Religious leaders could give advice," he said. "But they have no power to take decisions. The decisions are always in the hands of the governments. So how can they be changed, if not by having a new juridical form, legalizing a common moral order." Like Manuel Ulloa, he wanted war to be pronounced a crime against humanity. "Producing arms and bombs should be put outside the law."

Nothing as strong as this was in the declaration, though Carl Sagan did manage to get included a statement about action. The final version of the declaration looked like this:

FOR GLOBAL SURVIVAL

We have met at Oxford bringing together our individual experience from the parliaments and religious traditions of the world—and from the media, the sciences, business, education and the arts. We were brought together by a common concern for global survival, and have entered into a new dialogue on our common future.

This meeting is a timely convergence of hearts, minds, and events. Human society is in a period of intense introspection, gripped by fear, uncertainty, and confusion. But we are challenged by new opportunities and encouraged by signs of hope.

We recognize that it is not only human survival but the survival of the whole planet, with all its interdependent forms of life, which is threatened. The Earth, as recent environmental evidence confirms, is delicately balanced and vulnerable. Each one of us must accept the responsibility to care for and protect the Earth, which is our home.

We have derived from our meeting a vivid awareness of the essential oneness of humanity, and also the realization that each human person has both a spiritual and a political dimension. We acknowledge the inadequacy of attitudes and institutions within all our traditions to deal with our present global crisis.

WE THEREFORE NOW AFFIRM OUR SHARED VISION OF SURVIVAL, AND WE COMMIT OURSELVES TO WORK FOR A FUNDAMENTALLY CHANGED AND BETTER WORLD. WE URGE THE LEADERS OF THE WORLD TO ADOPT NEW ATTITUDES AND TO IMPLEMENT NEW POLICIES BASED ON SUSTAINABILITY AND JUSTICE.

We have explored the nature of the relationship between political and religious life, and as parliamentarians and spiritual leaders we have agreed that we both need and desire to work together. We have spoken frankly of the care that must be taken to listen to and not exploit one another. We invite our brothers and sisters from the fields of education, journalism, the arts, and other channels of communication to become our partners as we begin to develop together concrete plans of action at all levels.

We have worked together to formulate specific proposals. These include:

1. At the global level we commit ourselves to choose and to promote styles of life which will sustain our earth, sky, and sea for future generations; if we are to have a common future, we must act as responsible world citizens as well as loyal citizens of a particular nation.

2. Where international or civic relationships are broken by conflict or injustice, we commit ourselves to promoting reconciliation and peace; if we are to achieve common security, we must dismantle arms, build trust, and join in the struggle to enhance the quality of human life.

3. Where opportunities for practical cooperation exist within nations or local communities, we shall avoid jealous competition and promote respectful and equal

partnerships of young and old, women and men, of people of all races, religions, traditional cultures, and political persuasions.

4. Where misunderstandings or ignorance keep us apart, we shall develop in both public and private sectors modes of education, communication, and dialogue, which can provide ethical and moral motivation and appropriate technical methods.

5. While we strive for basic human rights, which should be inspired by our religious teachings and safeguarded by our political systems, we shall also exercise our human duties as individuals and communities to protect our earth and to protect each other.

6. Three areas of present critical concern shall receive our special attention: elimination of the perils of nuclear and other armaments; realization of appropriate balances between resources and populations; and promotion of the well-being of vulnerable groups, particularly women and children.

In order to implement these proposals we shall support existing structures, such as the United Nations agencies, and shall promote at regional, national, and local levels all possible collaboration between spiritual leaders and parliamentarians. As participants in this Oxford Global Survival Conference, we commit ourselves to revive neglected ideals, revitalize useful structures, and, where necessary, devise at every level new ways to coordinate our work and improve our communication.

Each one of us has been changed by our Oxford experience. We have clarified our objectives and undertaken commitments that are irrevocable. We know that we will be continually tested. We pledge to share the positive results of this conference with all people. Let us do so together with determination, love, and compassion.

The high point of that last morning, and indeed one of the high points of the conference, came when Chief Oren Lyons, faithkeeper of the Onondaga Council, and Thomas Banyacya, elder of the Hopi nation, read aloud to us a letter written in 1855 by Chief Seattle to the president of the U.S. in response to a commercial proposition: the white Americans wanted to buy the Indians' land. The letter went as follows:

How can one buy or sell the air, the warmth of the land? That is difficult for us to imagine. We do not own the sweet air or the sparkle on the water. How then can you buy them from us?

Each pine tree shining in the sun, each sandy beach, the mist hanging in the dark woods, every space, each humming bee, every part of the Earth is sacred to my people, holy in their memory and experience.

We are part of the Earth and the Earth is part of us. The fragrant flowers are our sisters. The reindeer, the horse, the great eagle are our brothers. The rocky heights, the foamy crests of waves in the river, the sap of meadow flowers, the body heat of the pony—and of human beings—all belong to the same family.

So when the Great Chief in Washington sends word that he wants to buy our land, he asks a great deal of us.

We know that the White Man does not understand our way of life. To him, one piece of land is much like another. He is a stranger who comes in the night and takes from the land whatever he needs. The Earth is not his friend but his enemy, and when he has conquered it, he moves on. He cares nothing for the land. He forgets his parents' graves and his children's heritage. He kidnaps the Earth from his children. He treats his Mother the Earth and his Brother the Sky like merchandise. His hunger will eat the Earth bare and leave only a desert.

I have seen a thousand buffalo left behind by the White Man—shot from a passing train. I am a savage and cannot understand why the puffing iron horse should be more important than the buffalo, which we kill only in order to stay alive. What are human beings without animals? If all the animals cease to exist, human beings would die of a great loneliness of the spirit. For whatever happens to the animals will happen soon to all human beings. Continue to soil your bed and one night you will suffocate in your own waste.

Humankind has not woven the web of life. We are but one thread within it. Whatever we do to the web, we do to ourselves. All things are bound together. All things connect. Whatever befalls the Earth befalls also the children of the Earth.

The letter had obviously been written by a man who did not feel himself to be an observer of a world outside him, but felt coursing in his blood the connectedness of everything on Earth, a man who reverenced the value of every form of life, including the planet herself. It formed a fitting end to a week where we had come to know our place in the web of life.

Index of Personal Names

About the Author

Anuradha Vittachi, a Sri Lankan writer, editor, and psychotherapist, was educated at Oxford University and now lives in London.

ALSO IN NEW SCIENCE LIBRARY

Awakening the Heart: East/West Approaches to Psychotherapy and the Healing Relationship, edited by John Welwood.

Between Time and Eternity, by Ilya Prigogine and Isabelle Stengers. (Forthcoming)

Fisherman's Guide: A Systems Approach to Creativity and Organization, by Robert Campbell.

The Holographic Paradigm and Other Paradoxes: Exploring the Leading Edge of Science, edited by Ken Wilber.

Imagery in Healing: Shamanism and Modern Medicine, by Jeanne Achterberg.

Order Out of Chaos: Man's New Dialogue with Nature, by Ilya Prigogine and Isabelle Stengers.

The Second Medical Revolution: From Biomedicine to Infomedicine, by Laurence Foss and Kenneth Rothenberg.

Space, Time and Medicine, by Larry Dossey, M.D.

Transformations of Consciousness: Conventional and Contemplative Perspectives on Development, by Ken Wilber, Jack Englar, and Daniel P. Brown.

Waking Up: Overcoming the Obstacles to Human Potential, by Charles T. Tart.

COGNITIVE SCIENCE

Brain, Symbol, and Experience: Toward a Neurophenomenology of Human Consciousness, by Charles L. Laughlin, Jr., John McManus, and Eugene G. d'Aquili. (Forthcoming)

Shifting Worlds, Changing Minds: Where the Sciences and Buddhism Meet, by Jeremy W. Hayward.

The Sphinx and the Rainbow: Brain, Mind and Future Vision, by David Loye.

The Tree of Knowledge: The Biological Roots of Human Understanding by Humberto R. Maturana and Francisco J. Varela.

The Wonder of Being Human: Our Brain and Our Mind, by Sir John Eccles and Daniel N. Robinson.

SCIENCE AND SPIRITUALITY

Choosing Reality: A Contemplative View of Physics and the Mind, by B. Alan Wallace.

Perceiving Ordinary Magic: Science and Intuitive Wisdom, by Jeremy W. Hayward.

Quantum Questions: Mystical Writings of the World's Great Physicists, edited by Ken Wilber.

Ritual and the Socialized Mind, by Henry M. Vyner. *(Forthcoming)*

Science and Creation: The Search for Understanding, by John Polkinghorne.

Science and Providence: God's Interaction with the World, by John Polkinghorne.

The Tao of Physics: An Exploration of the Parallels between Modern Physics and Eastern Mysticism, second edition, revised and updated, by Fritjof Capra.

Up from Eden: A Transpersonal View of Human Evolution, by Ken Wilber.

ECOLOGY AND GLOBAL CONCERNS

Evolution: The Grand Synthesis, by Ervin Laszlo.

The New Biology: Discovering the Wisdom in Nature, by Robert Augros and George Stanciu.

Staying Alive: The Psychology of Human Survival, by Roger Walsh, M.D.

Toward a Transpersonal Ecology, by Warwick Fox. *(Forthcoming)*